Sarkis Atamian
DOUGLAS AVENUE
Adventures of Douglas Avenue's Bad Boys

Foreword by Alison Atamian

Publication Consultants — Since 1978

PO Box 221974 Anchorage, Alaska 99522-1974
www.publicationconsultants.com

ISBN 978-1-59433-033-9
eBook ISBN 978-1-59433-114-5

Library of Congress Catalog Card Number: 2005908077

Copyright 2005 by Sarkis Atamian
—First Edition—

All rights reserved, including the right of reproduction in any form, or by any mechanical or electronic means including photocopying or recording, or by any information storage or retrieval system, in whole or in part in any form, and in any case not without the written permission of the author and publisher.

Manufactured in the United States of America.

Dedication

In dedication to the memory of Margaret Swensen, whose laughter at some of these stories got this book started.

Other books by Sarkis Atamian

The Bears of Manley

The Origin of Tarzan

Acknowledgments

I acknowledge with great gratitude, Evan and Lois Swensen for their help in making possible the publication of *Douglas Avenue*, Marthy Johnson who edited the manuscript, and my wife, Alison, the angel in disguise, who did the typing and made dinner on time every time.

Also, I must acknowledge my boyhood chums who were an inspiration for this book.

Foreword
by Alison Atamian

Four years ago, Sarkis suffered life-threatening injuries in a car accident. After a three-month stay in the hospital, he returned home, where he exerted himself in a determined effort to regain his strength. During this period, Sarkis' friend and publisher, Evan Swensen, encouraged him to begin writing *Douglas Avenue*. Struggling with pain and fatigue, Sarkis often found it discouraging to work on his manuscript. However, he persevered and his stories of *Douglas Avenue*, a book for which his boyhood chums were an inspiration, provide a glimpse into the lives of Armenian children, "growing up in families that struggled to overcome adversity and prosper, buoyed by love for one another and a sense of hope."

As a boy, Sarkis often heard his mother say of someone, "He has dropped something in his suitcase and is carrying it around." She meant by this that someone had an idea or story which they couldn't resist repeatedly sharing with anyone who would listen. Well, all of us, no doubt, cherish the memory of some experience we are eager to repeatedly pull out, dust off and tell. Perhaps a story is told with tenderness or humor, and punctuated with laughter, and yet another story we may remember with grief or regret, as our eyes well with tears. Sarkis was a wonderful storyteller and he could bring to life a moment from the past, eliciting laughter or tears from his audience, as he took captive each listener's imagination.

Do we not share our stories of joyful memories of success, survival, and of our celebrations of life with greater appreciation as time passes? If this is so, it may be that we perceive our experiences as having been significant, extraordinary or wondrous in a sense we did not fully appreciate when we first lived them. Sometimes we recognize belatedly that certain events were pivotal in the unfolding history of our lives. Our personal stories of tragedy, or poverty or of other anguish, may be understood in a new light, as having been instrumental in bringing families closer together, or having strengthened the bonds of friendship, or having taught lessons in life—of perseverance, humility, commitment, or self-reliance. Sarkis brings to life just such stories as he writes about the trials and triumphs of the Stepanian family of Douglas Avenue. Hope, faith and love flourish in this immigrant Armenian family's life. Mariam Stepanian, expresses this sense of hope when she proclaims, "This is truly a land of milk and honey. Thank God, our children have a promising future."

In the chapter, "Picnic Armenian Style", the Stepanian family joins others in the community for a Sunday afternoon picnic. It has been organized by those who survived the massacres from the Pavlu region in the old country. Everyone enjoys music, dancing, shish kebob, and many speeches, until daylight wanes. It has "been a typical Sunday of freedom from the worries and anxieties about the coming week, an opportunity to regain their strength to fight for life…" In conclusion, Sarkis wrote, "After all, these were the people who had survived the last attempt to wipe them off the earth's surface. The more their enemies or adversity threatened to wipe them out, the harder they lived to survive…today the children and grandchildren of that earlier generation thrive and take with them into the future the wealth of their Armenian inheritance."

In our collective storytelling, we pass on the values, traditions and history of a people. In an article written years ago, Sarkis reminisced about his participation as a young adult in the Armenian Youth Federation Olympics, saying, "What gave us a sense of purpose, pride, self-respect, and gratitude were the values and heritage of our people. These found their articulation for young minds in athletic events focused on the AYF Olympics." Later in the same article, Sarkis declared, "I know who I am and where I am going, no matter where this world claims me. I have no identity crisis."

Sarkis would often remind me that when you leave this life you take only your memories with you. He passed away on December 27, 2005, just weeks after approving the final draft for his book. In *Douglas Avenue*, Sarkis shares his collection of memories, about what it was like for youngsters of his generation to grow up in the Armenian community of Douglas Avenue. No doubt his contemporaries will recall their own special memories of childhood as they read the book, and certainly for the rest of us, Armenian or otherwise, we will take our own trip into the past.

The phrase, "Once there was and there was not" serves as the introduction to many an Armenian tale. It is the equivalent of beginning a story with, "Once upon a time." So I invite you to begin the journey back in time to once there was and there was not, on Douglas Avenue, an immigrant Armenian family, the Stepanians, whose children grew up during the Great Depression.

Dearest Sarkis, my beloved husband, may God illumine your soul.

Alison Atamian
Wasilla, Alaska
July 12, 2006

Contents

Dedication 3
Acknowledgments 4
Foreword 5
Introduction 9
Chapter 1 .... Crushing of the Grapes 11
Chapter 2 .... Cornfield Ghosts 19
Chapter 3 .... Counterfeit Money 25
Chapter 4 .... Washington's Cherry Tree 29
Chapter 5 .... Harry's Subconscious 35
Chapter 6 .... A Very Merry Christmas 41
Chapter 7 .... Chestnut Trophies 47
Chapter 8 .... On the Count of Three 49
Chapter 9 .... Leonard's Pond 55
Chapter 10 ...... Foul Ball 61
Chapter 11 ...... A Disreputable Man 63
Chapter 12 ...... No Tigers in Africa 79
Chapter 13 ...... The Untutored Peasant 84
Chapter 14 ...... The Green Snake 87
Chapter 15 ...... Honor Thy Family 90
Chapter 16 ...... Aerial Combat 97
Chapter 17 ...... Picnic Armenian Style 103
Chapter 18 ...... The Skeletal Horse 109
Chapter 19 ...... The First Round 115
Chapter 20 ...... Tony's Spaghetti Parlor 118
Chapter 21 ...... The Nickel Shoe Shine 123

Introduction

Providence, Rhode Island, was founded about 1636 by Roger Williams, a victim of religious persecution. Ever since, it has become a haven for successive arrivals, hoping to establish a better life for themselves and their families.

The earliest immigrants were English, French, Scandinavians, Germans, and other western Europeans. During and after World War I, the nation opened its doors to the Irish, Poles, Russians, Lithuanians, Jews, Greeks, Italians and the rest of the "huddled masses" which included, last but not least, the Armenians. Many of these people gravitated to Providence, Rhode Island.

Having suffered the first and worst genocide of the 20th century at the hands of the Ottoman Turks, Armenians arrived not for economic advantage but for sheer survival as remnants of a devastated nation and culture. America was the kindest place to be. The first substantial settlements were in New England, especially in Providence, Rhode Island.

These newcomers found that New England winters can be bitterly cold, and discovered that summers are hot and humid but are often delightfully cooled by the offshore breezes from Narraganset Bay. They marveled at the beauty of fall, when the foliage of hardwood trees turned orange, yellow, gold, and brown, creating a magical image, as though van Gogh had just been there with his palette, mixing his fantastic colors.

By the early 1920s, Providence had long since become an important manufacturing center of industrial equipment, machine tooling, jewelry, and sundry things. A variety of fish and other seafood was harvested from an Atlantic cornucopia. The immigrants sought employment in this environment.

In Providence, early ethnic communities were squeezed together on Smith Hill in an area including Douglas Avenue, Charles, Ormes, and Eaton Streets. Many Armenians settled into an enclave which began on Douglas Avenue. It was one of the oldest parts of the city, situated along the top of Smith Hill. Douglas Avenue ran from the top of Smith Hill into the North

Providence area. The hill was scarcely a couple of miles from the state capitol building, reputed to be one of the most beautiful in the nation. Charles Street, then Ormes Street, followed by Eaton Street, rolled down the hill toward the center of town.

On Douglas Avenue the Jewish synagogue, which still exists today, was located across the street from some bakeries, delicatessen stores, and a kosher meat market. These were all within a block or two which also contained several Armenian homes. Further along the street, Armenian homes increased in number as the community expanded, taking up the next couple of miles. Surrounding the Armenian enclave were the ethnic communities of Russian, Polish, Lithuanian, and Irish immigrants. Then began Eaton Street running up past the Dominican College and downhill into the Italian enclave.

It is ironic that in those days all these ethnic neighborhoods left each other alone based on what was known by the earlier sociologists as the "consciousness of kind." A person lived in a real community without the benefit of welfare programs. It was only later that politics began a coercive drive to create a "multiculturalism" which resulted in the alienation of the individual from his rootedness. The person became a little bit of every other culture by losing most of his own. But in earlier days, immigrants clung tenaciously to the only thing they really owned: their identity.

When the Great Depression of the 1930s descended on the nation, Armenians suffered greatly. Their children, born in this country, grew up with all the problems of any first generation experiencing cultural marginality.

Armenians cherished one joy above all others: their children. Growing up in the Great Depression, these children provided their parents with the will and courage to survive despite all odds. The stories of *Douglas Avenue* provide a glimpse into the lives of some of these youngsters growing up in families that struggled to overcome adversity and prosper, buoyed by love for one another and a sense of hope. These are the good and bad times one family, the Stepanians, lived through during those days of becoming Americans.

Chapter 1
Crushing of the Grapes

The immigrant community of Armenian parents could understand the strange American world around them largely through what they could observe in their children's behavior. On the other hand, they did their best to discourage their kids from speaking English at home. These parents were caught in a double bind. Turkish politics had committed genocide against the Armenians during World War I and those who survived or escaped by some miracle reached the American shore virtually penniless. Obviously, they understood the foreign world around them with difficulty. Consequently, they insisted their children speak Armenian at home in order to maintain their native culture and only language the parents could understand.

During the Great Depression of the 1930s many Americans were hard hit but among ethnic peoples Armenians may have been harder hit than most. Competition made it more difficult for an average Armenian to find work even as a common laborer. He knew practically no English and could be easily identified as a foreigner, even from a distance: he looked Armenian because the men sported large prominent noses, bushy eyebrows, and large, curly handlebar mustaches if they came from the peasant hinterland. All one had to do was take one look at these hardy folks to be immediately imprinted with the imagery like an electronic terminal board.

Though many of them opened up a business of some kind, many more worked in factories. It cost twenty–five cents a month to send the kids to Armenian school, paid for by a hard–working father who did any kind of labor to keep his family going if he was lucky enough to find a job. The mother virtually commanded the household and left the discipline to the father, giving him the mistaken notion that he called the other shots, too.

As immigrants in the early 1920s, Dickron and Mariam Stepanian settled in Providence, Rhode Island. They established themselves in the Armenian neighborhood of Douglas Avenue. Within a few years, the couple were proud parents of two sons, Garo and Harootyoun. The brothers were close in age and so shared most of their boyhood adventures.

Garo and Harootyoun, like other Armenian children born in this country, were often reprimanded for using English at home, their parents insisting that only Armenian should be spoken. Some parents, Dickron and Mariam among them, who as children had learned Turkish in the old country, occasionally used it in this country in the presence of their children. That's how the kids in the new country knew that they had a multicultural problem of a different sort. Whenever parents or older Armenians spoke in Turkish, their children knew that the subject was about forbidden things such as sex, which they suspected without understanding. The subject was taboo. Teasing their parents, children would exclaim, "In Armenian, please," and run away before parents realized their mistake.

Garo had asked his father fairly early in his young life why some of the old-timers spoke Turkish, imported from the old school of their childhood. Most immigrants' kids could recognize it as such, even though they could not understand a word of it. Once, when Garo asked why fathers could slip into Turkish while their sons could not use English at home, Poppa had instantly jumped to his feet. "That's different," he said.

"Why?" Garo asked, incautiously.

In reply, Poppa asserted, "That's because we are a clean and moral people; we have no profanity in our Armenian language. When we have to use forbidden words we borrow from you know what language. You are not allowed to use forbidden words. Do you understand?" Garo understood instantly and he quickly moved out of range as he saw his father eyeing his razor strop.

After ten years in America, living with her family in the isolation of the Armenian enclave, Mariam Stepanian's English was still too broken. On the few occasions when she had attempted to speak English in order to communicate with the *odars* or foreigners, as she called English-speaking Americans, she'd been told, "Hey, talk American."

Like most Armenian mothers, she commandeered huge chunks of the fatherly role except when the going was too tough and she could dump it on Poppa's lap. One of Momma's main tasks was the education of her children. She taught her sons to respect their parents and elders. For example, they were to address older or married women as *Deegeen*, except their mother, of course. It was a formal and elegant way to address women. Momma's was a wiser kind of thought control before multiculturalism would later applaud the dumbing-down theory.

If the brothers talked about their parents, shared their secrets, or told off-color street jokes, it was done beyond earshot. Certain four-letter words, later to be commonplace on television as an advancement of free speech, were outlawed at home and in school at that time.

Shortly after the fall semester began in school, the language problem occurred when the Stepanian's younger son, Harootyoun, started school. His name meant "resurrection." Many Armenian names were loaded with Christian references since Armenia was the first nation, worldwide, to officially adopt that faith in A.D. 301. However, their son rebelled against any church teaching, even before he finished kindergarten, on the grounds that his classmates could never accept anything which sounded like "Harootyoun." They were having too much fun deliberately mispronouncing his first name.

The school psychologist said the kid was suffering from doubt about his identity or from what would be described in later years, as an "identity crisis." The entire enclave heard about that and asked, "What the hell does that mean?" Fathers, especially, laughed at that one since they felt they had one of those—whatever it meant—every other day.

When news got out and was distributed around the enclave, the school's diagnosis was rejected on the grounds that the virenees (wilderness people) in charge of the school system must not believe in the soul and therefore could not know anything about its spirit. Late one afternoon, Harootyoun was reported missing from school. The police found the runaway a couple of miles from home walking in the wrong direction. He didn't know about identity crises but he knew how he felt every time the non-Armenians tried to pronounce his name the non-Armenian way. He was happy about being himself and didn't want anyone else's identity, whatever an identity was.

Momma and Poppa finally had his name changed to Harry, an Anglicized version of his Armenian name, because it was easy to pronounce and sounded American. After that, his teachers seemed to smile at him more often, though his classmates scowled at the killjoy.

One afternoon, after school let out, the boys were playing peggy. The peg was a stub of broom handle about eight inches long, tapered at both ends. A longer section of the broom handle, used as a bat, was swung sharply down to the tapered end of the smaller section lying on the ground. As the peg flew upward a couple of feet, it was swatted in midair as far as it would go. It was a popular game, the only trouble being the sudden increase in the number of broken windows from one neighborhood to the next. One always knew when the season began because of the increase in sales of glass panes at the hardware store. Once, Harry hit a beauty which sailed across three back yards and landed without steam on the sidewalk just as Deegeen Carian crossed the street. She was a garrulous and acerbic old woman, a neighbor who lived in the tenement above the Stepanian's. For Harry, it was an insult to demean the word *Deegeen* in Deegeen Carian's case, since there was little dignified or elegant about her manners, speech, or behavior. She had never lost her provincial habits.

She had just crossed the street, going home, when the peggy Harry had swatted so mightily landed and bounced once or twice and thumped against Deegeen's Carian billowing skirt, which stopped the peggy cold. It rolled off harmlessly. However, she stumbled and hopped like a vaudevillian as though she had broken both femurs, until the kids broke out laughing once they saw through her act.

Taking offense at the ridicule, she immediately hobbled to Deegeen Mariam's door, hammered on it furiously until it was opened and Mariam stood in the doorway, sensing the worst. "Look at what the monsters you call your children did to me," Deegeen Carian complained.

Rather than accept Mariam's apologies for whatever had happened and accept her invitation to enter, she gloated upon seeing the latter's embarrassment and emptied herself of her vitriol. She was satisfied only when she slammed the door shut in her landlady's face and nicely walked upstairs.

Mariam knew that Deegeen Carian's hostility resided in her envy or jealousy for not having children of her own when all the other immigrant married women in the neighborhood had lots of them. Yet it could not be denied that the well–spent peggy had touched Deegeen Carian's skirt, no matter how lightly. Harry had shouted an abbreviated cry of joy but quickly choked it off when he realized what he had done, but it was too late.

When Mariam's husband, Dickron, got home from his temporary job he washed away the grime and dirt from the workshop and had dinner, after which he gently asked his wife what had happened. That something had happened was obvious from his wife's behavior. She repeated the story about the boys' peggy game and the peg which had glanced off Deegeen Carian's voluminous and heavy skirt. Father and sons had a one–sided communication about it.

To relieve herself of her anger, Deegeen Carian thought about crushing her two 28–pound boxes of overripe grapes for the season's wine. The old–country custom of stepping on them with bare feet in a large container was the most practical way of doing that, and she had always found the mashing of luscious grapes gave her a soothing feeling.

She had left the grapes in their boxes on top of the stairs to the second floor. The crushing could begin in a day or two. In the meantime, she and her husband, Toross, had gone to the neighbors' to play Scambil, a favorite card game from the old country. (No one was home.)

Harry stumbled over the boxes when he climbed to the attic, but paid them no mind. He was looking out of the window to see if a mother pigeon had returned to her nest under one of the eaves, but there was no sign of her. On his way down, he stopped to take a good look at the two boxes of grapes and he knew that the Carians had gone out, which was why the grapes had not been taken inside. They looked too luscious for him not to take a few so he helped himself to a bunch and that's when Satan "dropped it into his mind," as they said in the old country. Harry yelled to his brother to come upstairs, since he needed some assistance in helping Satan, who never needed it.

Harry had seen Deegeen Carian crushing grapes by stepping on them barefooted. He could think of no reason why he couldn't do just as good a job himself using the same technique and saving Deegeen Carian the trouble, which he gladly took on for himself. He removed his fire–sale Thom McCann shoes and socks. Garo, who only wanted to eat a few of the grapes, moaned, "You don't mean..."

"Yeah. I do," said Harry. "Remember how last month she complained to Poppa about our being 'little devils' and made Momma cry? What's more, Poppa spanked us, even if his heart was not in it. You said we had to get even with Deegeen Carian for that. Well, here's our chance. Are you gonna back out now?"

With that he jumped right into one grape mound and started stomping with maniacal vim and vigor, to borrow one of his music teacher's pet phrases. "Ya gonna jump in or just stand there and watch?" Harry chortled.

It was too much for Garo. He yanked off his Tom McCanns and socks and jumped in, too. Instantly, he felt the cool juice of the popping grapes ooze between his toes. Both brothers were now laughing uproariously and did not see the forthcoming consequences. In a few minutes Momma's voice cut through the overhead thumping sound to ask what was going on up there, and yelled for it to stop. The boys knew that their world was about to change.

They grabbed their shoes and socks and rushed back downstairs. They turned on the hose pipe in the backyard, wiped their feet dry with a towel from the clothesline, went into the house and listened to the radio as Tom Mix of the Ralston Straight Shooters was out-shooting the bad guys. Momma looked at her boys with suspicion, knowing something bad had happened. The boys didn't know when the inquisition would begin.

Some time later, there was a knock on the door and when Mariam saw Deegeen Carian's scowling face, she instantly knew that something was wrong indeed. Her voice trembled when she said she couldn't understand her tenant's rapid–fire, machine–gun tirade, and invited the half–crazed woman to come in, have a seat, and explain what had happened. The hysterical woman only redoubled the onslaught, grabbing

Mariam by the arm and screaming, "You want to know what happened? You really want to know what happened? Come, I'll show you what happened." She dragged Mariam by the arm to the landing of the stairs. "Do you see that, do you see that?" she yelled, pointing to the wet, shiny surface of the trickled grape juice which ran a trail down to the bottom step and landing.

"That's my grape juice, my grape juice! Do you see what your monsters have done?" In vain Mariam tried to mollify her and by putting together some of the words, she sensed the rest of the story. She promised her husband would pay for what her monstrous children had done and hurried into the safety of her kitchen.

Shortly after the madwoman had stopped her diatribe and gone upstairs, the man of the house walked in and before he had taken half a step inside, he stopped. Something was wrong. "What's this sticky stuff on the floor?" he asked his wife and tried to scrape it off his shoes. Mariam could not hold it in any longer and broke into tears. She went inside, turned on the water for her husband's wash and helped him clean up while he tried to calm her down. Then they sat for dinner and she went into details.

"Dearest woman," he said, "everything will be all right. Please, no more tears." After dinner, he went upstairs to make things all right. He called Toross Carian to the door and assured him he would be paid for all costs, apologized for what the boys had done, and asked what Deegeen Carian had paid for the grapes. She, of course, could smell victory, so she instantly hollered from behind the closed door, "Three dollars!"

It sounded like half a week's wages to Dickron but he said loudly enough so that his wife, Mariam, would hear from his side of the closed door, "Well, that's fair enough." He hoped that she was forewarned so as to soften the shock, before he had to tell her face to face. After all, she was the bookkeeper in the family. He also knew that Mr. Toross was embarrassed by his wife's piracy so he asked him, *sotto voce*, "If I take three dollars and fifty cents off next month's rental now, will you accept it?"

Mr. Toross stood in silent surprise for a moment, realizing this was too unfair for his landlord but before he could answer, his wife, still behind the door, shouted, "Yes, yes, we will accept it!" Mr. Toross, blushing with shame at his wife's indiscretion, reached out to shake hands and the deal was set.

"Dearest woman, don't worry, everything will be all right," Dickron said again on his return to the kitchen and told his wife about the agreement he and Toross had reached. She wanted so much to reach out and hug her man but this wasn't done in the presence of their children. To the surprise of the kids, their father did not seem really angry. Instead, he asked, "Boys, do you know how you have really shamed your mother and father?"

"I'm sorry, Poppa," Garo said.

"I am, too," Harry said. Both had shamefully bowed their heads and when they silently looked up, their eyes filled with tears and the boys did not cry often. They kissed the back of the hand that Poppa extended to them, with the older brother going first. It was a sign of the deep respect boys paid their father when they knew how badly they had hurt his feelings, and without words he was saying they had been forgiven. Then they all hugged each other, with Momma sharing the honors first. The family had won the odds over the devil again.

Chapter 2
Cornfield Ghosts

One day, Mariam Stepanian received a letter postmarked from France! She could not read the sender's cursive writing on the envelope and, somewhat mystified, she opened the letter nervously and stood breathless for a moment. It was in Armenian from Professor Zartarian! Memories flooded back. The professor had been Mariam's schoolteacher just before the Turkish genocide of the Armenians began in 1915. It had thrown the terrified population into panic and mass confusion in Adapazar, separating families from each other and children from their parents. Mariam's father had taken his children and left them with relatives living elsewhere. Mariam and an uncle had managed to survive and made their way to America, where Mariam had married early.

Professor Zartarian arrived in America after World War I. One of the first things she did, like so many of her people, was to check with the Armenian relief societies, searching for relatives, survivors, and others from her hometown of Adapazar, which was a coastal city far from the hinterland. She discovered four families with the same surname of Terchunian. One of them sounded very much like the name of a former pupil's uncle. The professor's letter was answered, whereby she learned that the recipient knew of a Terchunian who had come to America from Adapazar. The professor wrote to the addressee and learned that she knew of a Terchunian who had moved to Providence, Rhode Island. Professor Zartarian wrote to that address and it was Mariam who had received her former teacher's letter!

Such chain letters were becoming commonplace throughout America where uprooted survivors were searching for each other. The letter from the professor was a tremendous lift to Mariam's morale. It came at a time when all America, maybe the whole world, was reeling from the Great Depression of the 1930s. Despite President Franklin D. Roosevelt's promises, the nation's economic recovery was slow in coming and in many cases never came at all. Immigrants from many European nations were flooding American shores. Many of them came to escape poverty, but the Armenians came to escape genocide. They got a later start in this country than others. One thing they had in common with the West was Christianity but that hardly helped overcome the language barrier. The Armenian language did not use the alphabet common to the Romance languages of western European countries. Among some of the earlier arrivals from Christian cultures, prejudices and discrimination against Armenians intensified due to the increased pressure of rampant unemployment during the Depression.

Dickron Stepanian married Mariam Terchunian, who gave him their sons, Garo and Harry. He found a part–time job in an iron foundry, barely earning enough to keep his family going. His only recreation and relief from the grinding toil of the foundry was going to the men's Armenian Club on Saturday afternoons. It was a crowded place where card games and backgammon were played with passion. When he won, which was often, he brought home candy bars for the children and a cigar or two for himself as part of the winnings.

He returned home late one Saturday afternoon from the club to give his wife time to renew acquaintance with her former teacher. The professor's friends had left her at Mariam's, where the two reunited women shared their tears of joy and sorrow for things past. They sat for Armenian–style coffee, thick and brown, and the professor related what had happened in the years since her favorite pupil's departure.

Mariam had made some of the old–country pastry to honor her dear professor's visit but she was a bit on edge. She apologized for the small house and said to the professor, "It's not like the lovely home we had in Adapazar is it, but it's the best we can do." In fact, the entire house was too small, though spotlessly clean. The couch, or what passed for it, was pushed into a corner of the tiny main room with its wintertime coal–burning stove. This and two cramped bedrooms were all they had in the Depression's poverty. Mariam was feeling a shade of embarrassment because this house was home, but it was hardly the house she would have shown the professor in the old country. The professor was the essence of kindness and understanding. She, too, had survived the agony of her people and so they passed the afternoon with gratitude for what was still left to them by fate.

In the meantime, Garo and Harry returned from the playground and saw Deegeen Carian leaning over the fence of the backyard, chatting with her neighbor. The boys instinctively stepped back since Deegeen Carian still held onto her animosity from the grape–stomping episode. Crouching low, the boys squirmed to the edge of the garden. They were now in the middle of the cornfield. The field was small but the corn was high enough to serve as a perfect cover. That's when the idea occurred to both of them at almost the same instant. It was Harry who signaled a halt to their serpentine crawling through the stalks. Garo seemed a little winded and setting down the peggy swatter, signaled Harry for a brief stop.

They could hear, without too much strain, what the two women were chatting about—their favorite subject: Deegeen Mariam. Deegeen Carian was saying about her, in the peasant vernacular of her old–country village, "She thinks she is so smart with her citified language and manners."

"Worse than that," said her neighbor. "She thinks like all of her kind that they are better than we lowly peasants." Ethnically, the Deegeens Mariam and Carian had come from the same stock, but socially they belonged in two different worlds it seemed. And the differences went all the way from colloquialisms in the same language to schooling and lifestyles in the hinterland and the urban world.

"I don't like what they are saying about Momma," Harry said in a whisper to Garo and looked around for anything he could pelt them with. "Listen to that upstairs neighbor. What does she have against Momma?" he asked.

But Garo cautioned restraint. "If you hit her with anything after the peggy wallop, you know what Poppa will say to us. It would be better to show her that Momma is ten times the better woman than that *virenee*."

"How do you plan to do that?" Harry asked. "I want to get even now before I lose the urge."

Garo wondered how he could talk his kid brother out of what could be another disaster. He pulled Harry closer to him and whispered in his ear, "You want to get even with her, don't you?" Harry nodded assent. Garo needed an inspirational plan of action just then and it was Deegeen Carian who unwittingly provided it.

At that moment Deegeen Carian leaned over the fence a little more and it lifted her homemade, ankle–length skirt. "Do you see what she's wearing underneath?" Garo asked. "She's wearing a heavy woolen skirt because she thinks she's still in the mountainous countryside of her village in the old country, where it's really colder than here."

Harry looked at his brother suspiciously. "You're making that up, aren't you?" he asked.

"No I'm not," Garo said. In fact, he had referred to a real practice of dressing among peasant women, who layered their skirts for warmth against cold weather. Deegeen Carian shifted her foot just enough to reveal a second petticoat. The edge of the first petticoat then fell over the second one.

"I wonder how many of those skirts she wears?" Harry asked.

"There's one way to find out," Garo suggested.

Harry seemed about to ask another question. Garo signaled "Be still," and reached out for his peggy stick, but Harry instantly caught on and grabbed it first. Ever so carefully, he slid the tip of it under the second petticoat and lifted numbers one and two up together. Deegeen Carian reached to her backside without turning and slapped away what she thought was an errant corn stalk. The bulk of the imagined stalk was heavier now and Harry with a nudge signaled Garo to take his turn and pushed the stick over to him. Garo aligned the "engine of destruction." He caught the lower fold of the third skirt and passed the loaded bundle back, except that Harry failed to respond.

When Garo looked up to see what was holding things up— or down, in this case—he saw Harry convulsed with choked–off laughter so hard that both hands were cupped over his mouth. He seemed to be turning purple for lack of air. At that moment the weight of what now looked like a bundle of laundry became too much to handle. Instantly, Garo recognized the problem.

He had seen these ankle-length skirts of the old country before, hanging from second-story clotheslines. Deegeen Carian was wearing at least three or four of them, one over the other. Only this could explain the constant display of them snapping in the breeze on her clothesline, or so Garo reasoned.

Deegeen Carian felt something sliding up her leg again but absentmindedly brushed it off. Garo carefully passed the delicately balanced pile of cloth to his kid brother.

Harry lowered the load to the ground, pulled the stick out from beneath it and slipped it under the bottom of the heap again and lifted. He was turning blue again, trying to suffocate an uproarious laughter building up inside, as the loaded hems of the heavy skirts started swaying out of control. Deegeen Carian, without a backward glance, reached behind and swatted at the folds of her skirt again.

The cloth bundle required greater force to keep the now heavier weight on course. Accidentally, the bundle slipped and started to slide down her leg. To keep it on course it required just a tiny extra push which was just a hair too much. When the hapless victim sensed something terribly wrong, she turned around suddenly, which spilled the heavy mound of old-country wool to the ground. Maybe she thought they were demons from the underworld when two figures shot upwards as though from a cannon, gave nerve-shattering yells of victory, and took off faster than a flash of lightning. Deegeen Carian fell with a heavy thud to the ground but it was hard to tell whether she fainted or tripped over the folds of heavy Anatolian wool.

It did not take long for Deegeen Carian to regain her senses. She rushed to Deegeen Mariam's door and hammered on it. Mariam recognized the tempo instantly and moaned, "Oh, dear God, not now. Please, not now." She looked to see how Professor Zartarian was reacting, and moaned again.

The professor was astonished that Deegeen Carian had not even waited a second to be invited inside. She just threw the door open, stepped inside and screamed, "When will you stop your monsters from molesting me," and Mariam, who only wanted to fall through a hole in the floor, could not even finish her question and ask, "What now?"

Deegeen Carian was determined to finish her say. "You want to know what now? You have raised two monsters—two bastards. You want to know what they did? I'll tell you what they did. They grabbed a stick and tried to shove it up my ass," she screamed, then dashed out, slamming the door behind her.

Mariam had never been subjected to the vulgarity of such language (with Turkish words thrown in for good measure) and the crudity of such misbehavior. She fought back the tears of humiliation. And it all had to happen in the presence of such a friend and distinguished personage.

"Please, my daughter, don't cry. I understand. I really do." The professor had addressed Mariam as "my daughter," which was a term of endearment by older married women for younger women, out of respect for their womanhood. It took some doing before Mariam calmed down long enough to know she would never forget this moment.

What had been a hilarious prank for the boys ended as a torment of spirit for the gracious lady who was their mother and a poor peasant woman who could not see how she had been victimized by a capricious turn of fate guided by two pranksters.

Deegeen Carian told the tale of her calamity to anyone who would listen and before long the story had worked its way through the community. In her own way, she was getting even with Deegeen Mariam and her whole family. Each time she told her tale of woe to someone, she grew happier than the last time. There was always an added twist or turn to the tale and fairly soon it became several different versions of the same story. She swore that she had fallen into a large hole and was surrounded by mythical animals and she could name them: Demons, ghouls, and goblins and she described them as she thought she had really seen them.

Some years later on a cold, rainy day as the darkness began to fall, two young men were seen standing silently, with bowed heads. One of them spoke with a husky voice and talked over the gravestone. "We'll see you again next year. We are sorry for all the wrongs between us," said Garo.

"Dear Mrs. Carian," Harry said, "somehow you are more important to us now than before. We will not forget you. The whole world has changed, and so have we." Both of them kissed their fingertips and pressed them to the top of the headstone and each placed his flowers at the base of it. Slowly, they walked out to their car as Harry brushed away his tears.

Chapter 3
Counterfeit Money

There were problems which plagued Harry and they mostly were of a special category. They had to do with behavior which was right or wrong, good or bad, "do or don't do" situations.

One day he met one of the neighborhood kids in the *Ov kidna* store, one of the poorer small businesses in town. Roughly translated, it was called the "who knows?" store. If anyone asked where the store was which sold anything not sold elsewhere, he was always told to try there. At the moment, Harry's acquaintance was buying candy and Harry couldn't believe his ears as he listened in on the interchange between the boy and the store owner's wife. He heard her ask the kid if there was anything else he wanted and the kid said, "No, just charge it to my mother's account." The woman nodded, passed the bag of candy over the counter, the boy took it and walked out with his purchase.

Little Harry was dumbfounded. He had often heard his parents speak about the wonders of this "free country" and didn't quite understand it but he was certain he had just witnessed with his own eyes what freedom meant. Apparently all one had to do was ask for it and the store owner would put it in his hand.

The clerk noticed Harry standing by the counter and politely asked, "What can I get for you, young fellow?"

Not knowing anything about the necessity of money for making a purchase, Harry gave no thought to the fact that he hadn't a single coin in his pocket when he pointed to the animal crackers. Besides, hadn't saying the magical words, "charge it to my mother's account" been all that was necessary for the last customer to secure his bag of candy?

The woman asked, in Armenian, "You are Deegeen Mariam's boy, aren't you?" He nodded his assent. The lady knew right off to whom the boy belonged because she had often seen the child's mother walking with him and immediately recognized the boy as the Stepanians' younger son.

"That will be three cents," the woman continued as she placed the bag of animal crackers on the counter in front of Harry, while at the same time extending the palm of her other hand toward him, waiting patiently for Harry to hand over his coins.

Little Harry suddenly froze. Three cents?! If one kid could go into the store and walk out without having produced a cent, why shouldn't he? A brilliant thought occurred to him, and he acted upon it by saying, "Charge it to my mother's account."

The lady paused a moment but she was hurting for money like everyone else and with her welcoming charm was only too happy to add a new customer to her accounts. She could risk the chance of making a mistake.

"You're a very good boy," she said, thinking of his parents' good standing in the community. "You may take the cookies and I'll charge them to your mother's account." Surely this was a safe gamble, she thought to herself. The boy belonged to an honorable and trustworthy family. Nothing further need be considered.

Little Harry couldn't have imagined that the nice lady of the Ov Kidna store who had happily waited on him would wait another three or four weeks until she saw Mariam walking past the store's window. The nice lady hurried out the door, waylaid her, and in an angry voice asked, "How much longer must I wait before you pay me the three cents you owe me? Your son bought cookies on credit and your account is overdue!"

"I don't know what you are talking about," said Mariam, taken aback by the sudden verbal assault. "I'll check with my husband and boys. Maybe they know what you're talking about," she promised and hurriedly walked away.

Later in the day when her husband came home, Mariam told him of the day's events including the unpleasant encounter with the woman who had sold Harry the bag of cookies on credit. Dickron was shocked at first to learn of his son's wiliness but he soon felt a sense of secret pride and laughter coming on. "Well," he said, "the little rascal shows real talent, doesn't he?" and laughed heartily. "When you go by the store again, just go in and pay her. But first, we had better ask Harry for his side of the story."

After dinner, Harry was drawing cartoons when his mother

asked him to put his sketchpad aside because his father and she wanted to speak with him. Harry felt suspicious because of the tone of her voice.

Mariam cautiously got around to Harry's shopping at the Ov Kidna store. He admitted to the deed which he had really forgotten and apologized for it with bowed head. "Well," said his father with a shrug of his shoulders and a glance toward his wife, "I believe him. What do you think?" he asked his wife.

"I believe him, too," she said, "but I want you to tell him why it was wrong to do what he did."

Dickron took on his duty of providing another moral lecture, explaining why Harry's silence on the matter was wrong, that it was dishonest to charge a purchase without asking his mother. Harry apologized again without understanding exactly why, but he got the message. He wouldn't be charging anything in the future, without his parents' knowledge.

Harry's experience made him realize there was no substitute for a few coins in a fellow's pocket. But how did he come by the coins? One afternoon, he discussed his dilemma with a chum and was fascinated with his suggestion.

"Coins are made of silver, so let's make our own," his chum said.

"Make our own?" Harry asked incredulously as he recalled his father's recent lecture about the real ownership of money. "How are you gonna do that?"

"You wait a minute and I'll show you," his chum said and disappeared. When he returned in a few minutes he carried a couple of expired auto license plates and an iron file. "Now you just watch this," he said and began to file the edge of one of them. In a few moments he had it filed clean, shinny and bright and the filings formed a bright little silvery mound. "Now what color do you see?" he asked. "It's silver. Right?"

Harry was younger than his chum but smarter. "The color's changed but the metal underneath is still the same. It's not changed into glass, or salami, has it? And it ain't silver!"

"We gotta file a little deeper," his chum said.

"You file a little deeper until I work this pain out of my arm muscles. I think I got a pulled charley horse," Harry complained. His chum gave him a dirty look, not knowing whether to believe him but began to file deeper and faster until he had a notch cut down a bit deeper than an inch or so. Harry kept lowering his head to hide his grin, then his laughter. His chum worked his arms more and more slowly. Harry said, "Gee whiz, you've been at it for so long! I know I couldn't do it. Why don't you rest for a while?"

His chum looked up at him. "What are you trying to tell me, that I'm not strong enough?"

"Aw, no," Harry said, "I know how strong you are. Look at me," he said holding up his arm and partially flexing his bicep. "See, my muscle is smaller than yours."

"Maybe this ain't such a great idea, anyway. I don't know how we'd turn these silver powder filings into a nickel coin. I just didn't think that far ahead, I guess," Harry's chum grudgingly admitted.

"Well, we tried," Harry offered as a cover–up for his sense of guilt in having doubted the whole idea to begin with. "There's gotta be an easier way to make some money," he suggested hoping that it would do the trick. That's what he hoped but deep down he knew that his chum was often given to a wide variety of fantasies. This had to be one of them and he'd probably only come up with another one that was just as crazy.

"I tell ya what, why don't we call it a day," Harry suggested, adding, "We can get together tomorrow, maybe."

Harry's chum nodded in agreement, saying, "Okay, I'll see ya soon," and he gathered his license plates and file.

With relief, Harry rushed home. He quickly opened the door just as his mother was fumbling for the doorknob from the other side. She gasped with surprise when the door opened. "Oh, my God, you startled me so!"

"I'm sorry, Momma, I didn't know you were there," he said. He seemed so hurt for having startled his mother that he leaned over and hugged her.

She responded, murmuring, *Jig-gerus, yegoor, yegoor,* (in Armenian, "My liver, come, come.") and hugged him in her arms. Any Armenian mother would have spoken thus, since for Armenians, the liver, rather than the heart, is the seat of all emotion and passion.

"Where were you today, my son?"

"I was busy trying to make my own money, Momma."

Chapter 4
Washington's Cherry Tree

It was a lovely Friday afternoon. Dickron and two of his friends were seated in the front yard in the shade of a huge elm tree. There was a refreshing breeze which rustled the leaves of the elm as the men sipped their Armenian coffee. Engrossed in a political discussion, they paid no attention to an automobile coming down the street until it slowed to a stop nearby. The passenger rolled down her window and asked if this was where Garo Stepanian lived and if so, could she and her companion speak to him.

Dickron called to his son and asked him what the women wanted. Garo had already bolted down the porch steps and was heading toward their car. "They're my teachers, Poppa," he shouted, pausing a moment and then continuing. Dickron followed his son over to greet the ladies.

Miss Larkin explained that she and Miss Flannigan wanted to know if Garo's parents would grant him permission to be in a school pageant celebrating George Washington's birthday in a couple of weeks.

Garo translated their question for his father, who instructed Garo, "Tell them that it would be an honor for my son to be in such a play. And you must also tell her a very important truth about Mr. Washington which I bet she doesn't know. Shortly after the war of the American Revolution the first mention of Washington's name in Asia was in a newspaper report written by an Armenian publisher in India. Armenians knew about that great man long before many others did!"

When Garo dutifully translated everything his father had said, one of the teachers responded, "In fact, Mr. Stepanian, we have considered giving your son the part of young George

Washington. If he accepts the part, the first practice session will begin on Monday, after school."

"Yes! I want to be George Washington!" Garo exclaimed.

"That's settled then," replied Miss Larkin. "There's the matter of your costume. You'll need a pair of dark blue trousers, a white shirt, and a red necktie. Oh, and one more item, could you also find a hatchet because you'll be pretending to chop down the fabled cherry tree of Washington's boyhood?"

"Don't forget to tell your mother that practice begins after school on Monday and you'll be late coming home by about an hour," Miss Flannigan reminded Garo, as she and Miss Larkin got back in their car.

When Mariam called her family for dinner, Dickron announced the good news of Garo's selection for the pageant. He was so proud of his son that he choked up for a moment, then he began clapping his hands and his family joined him in the applause. "Can you imagine our son will play George Washington in an American school?" he asked his wife.

Later that evening when the boys were asleep Dickron considered how he could afford to purchase the clothing Garo would need for the play. "The only problem now is to raise the money," he said aloud.

"Don't worry," his wife reassured him. "I have already prayed about that."

Her husband said, "I know there is a haberdashery on North Main street and we can get there with a one–trolley car ride. Let's try it as soon as we can and see if we can get back before the children come home from school."

"We can go on Monday," she suggested, and disappeared for a few moments. She returned with a small packet, and tossing it on the table, said, "This is how we'll do it."

Dickron opened it and out slid a gold locket on a gold chain, and within the locket was a twenty–dollar American gold coin. "I've kept this all these years for an emergency," she said, "and certainly now is the time."

"Oh no!" Dickron remonstrated. "That is yours and I will not allow you to squander it." He frowned with disapproval.

"This is not squandering," she replied adamantly. "This is an emergency and I can't think of anything more important for our son, right now. Please, dearest man, let us do it."

For several moments Dickron sat with his head bowed and his hands cupped under his chin. Finally, he said, "Very well, I guess you are right."

Early Monday morning, they took the trolley car downtown to the mall and walked the rest of the way, getting off near the haberdashery. The salesman had the charm of all such salesmen and asked if he could help. Dickron said, "Yes, please. We look for young boy pants."

"How tall is he?"

"He come to here," Dickron said, running his hand across his shoulder.

"We want a dark blue color," Mariam added.

In a few moments the salesman returned and before he could say anything Mariam said, "No long pants. I want it here," and she slid her hand across her knees.

"Oh, I see," said the salesman and searched briefly before selecting what he thought might satisfy her specifications. Then he said, "These are not trousers. They are called knickers."

"Oh, I see. One minutes, please," said Mariam, and opening her purse, removed a tooth pick around which was wrapped some string. She placed the end of the string against the waistband of the knickers, unwinding the string down the length of the garment. The knot in the other end of the string, which she had previously tied when measuring Garo, came to rest on the kneeband of one gathered pant leg.

"Ah, ha," she said to the salesman, "This long very right, no?" she asked.

The salesman didn't laugh but his smile was just right, confirming her conclusion. Mariam then asked, "Where stockings is, please?" The salesman walked her to a counter where she rummaged until she found the ones to match the knickers.

"Now comes the big transaction," Dickron told his wife, as he took her by the arm and pulled her in front of him. "You do this better than I can. Give us one of your big smiles," he encouraged her.

She was surprised for a moment, but regained her composure and removing the gold coin from her purse, handed it to the salesman. For a moment, he stared with amazement at the small fortune he held in his hand. Then as he started to walk away, Mariam's hand shot out like a bolt of lightning.

She grabbed him by the arm and said, "One minutes, please. Where you go?"

"I'm going to see my manager for his approval to return your change. It is a large amount," he said. "I'm sorry, but it is required by management." Suddenly, the problem dawned on him. She was nervous about losing sight of him and the money.

"What is he saying?" she asked her husband in Armenian, which the salesman could not understand, of course. But from the change in her voice and expression the salesman suspected what was wrong. The thought of losing a sale was more than a little disturbing so he hastened to reassure her. He placed the gold coin in the husband's hand, bowed and said to her, "Madame, won't you please follow us?" He ushered them to the manager's office where he stepped aside, holding the door open for husband and wife to enter first. They were then invited to be seated.

The salesman described the problem for the manager who took the sales slip, added the figures and said to husband and wife, "Your bill is three dollars and fifty cents. I want you to be our good customers so just give me three dollars. We will give you your change in paper money. Is that all right?" He looked inquiringly at Mariam. "Madame, I just want you to be happy."

"What is he saying now?" Mariam asked her man.

Her man, with a broad smile, said to his wife, "He wants you to be happy so he's giving you a discount."

"Oh," she said to the manager, with a big smile, "You good man. T'ank you very much. And you too," she said to the salesman. "I sorry I give you all too much trouble."

"No, no" the manager said, "no trouble at all. Thank you and please come again."

As man and wife walked back to the trolley stop, he said to her, "You looked so worried about the salesman. What bothered you about him?"

"He was too agreeable. I forgot for a moment that we weren't in the old country. Back there, we would have bargained for half an hour. It was hard to tell today, who got the better part of the deal," she responded.

"Yes, but look at how the manager gave us a break on the price. We might have walked all over town searching for a better bargain, only to find the next crook might have been less generous." Dickron smiled and gripped her hand more tightly for a moment. "You miss haggling as you once did in the old country bazaar but don't forget it was patrolled by a Turkish soldier and his presence was unnerving. I remember one day when I was shopping in the bazaar and witnessed a Turkish vendor call a soldier over to his stall to intervene with an Armenian customer who bargained too well. The customer was informed that he could either pay the vendor's price or go away empty-handed."

Mariam nodded. A few moments later, she hesitantly inquired, "what shall we do with the remaining money?"

"Settle our outstanding bill with the grocer," Dickron replied, "and then we'll think about what to do with the rest of the money if there's any left over. Right now, if we hurry to catch the trolley in time, we can beat the children home from school."

The day of the pageant rolled around soon enough. After the introductions and speeches were over, the pupils, all sixteen of them, self-consciously marched in single file to their positions on the stage and faced their audience. The program began. Each pupil spoke his or her few lines and bowed for the applause. Garo was fourth in line. "There is our Garo," his mother whispered with pride, unable to hold back her tears. "Do you see him? Do you?" she asked again.

"Yes, I see him," his father replied proudly.

Garo was standing stiffly erect, holding his hatchet at an angle across his chest as he declared, "I am George Washington, the Father of my Country and I cannot tell a lie. I chopped down the cherry tree." He bowed and as he straightened up, his hatchet slipped from his hand. Garo reflexively jumped backward as it fell, jerking his foot out of harm's way just as the hatchet hit the wooden floor with a loud thud. It looked so real that some in the auditorium gasped in fright while others roared in laughter. Garo bent over and picked up the plaster hatchet which had broken in its fall. He snapped to attention, took his bow and kept a straight face. The audience applauded the aplomb with which young "George" brought off the pretense. It took a while before the laughter and applause died down while young "George" bowed again and again as long as the director, backstage, kept waving her hands for more.

Never intended nor foreseen, this moment was the highlight of the evening. "George" had stolen the show.

When the event came to a close and the crowd had dispersed, Garo and his parents had but a short distance to walk on their way home. His admiring parents gave Garo hugs and kisses. His father asked what made his son think of his impromptu ending. Garo, throwing up his hands, said, "I was so embarrassed I didn't know what else to do."

"You did just fine, Son," his mother and father proudly assured him.

Chapter 5
Harry's Subconscious

Mariam used a large three-foot galvanized metal tub for the weekend bathing of the children when the plumbing in the bathroom had frozen. The tub was also used as a temporary boiler for the laundry where a washboard and yellow homemade soap were used to scrub the clothes sparkling clean as radio advertisements used to say.

The tub was also used for heavy-duty washing of flour sacks. At regular intervals the boys were sent out on a shopping detail. They would visit the local bakeries and if they were lucky in their timing they could buy two or three empty flour sacks for a dime each. Mariam, with her genius on the treadle sewing machine, made all sorts of things for home use with these sacks after ripping the seams open and laundering them. When it came to specialty items she shopped carefully in the downtown stores for fabrics on sale. She bought clothes only when necessary, which was not often. This was standard practice for many women during those Depression years.

Mariam was in the middle of her sewing one afternoon when Harry got home from school later than usual. She was not surprised, however, since pupils had been advised by home room teachers to notify their parents that the school doctors would be making annual routine physical examinations. Armenian parents, especially, were delighted and humbled with gratitude for this free public service, which they could not afford otherwise. "This is the land of Canaan," Mariam always said for such a blessing.

In due time Harry went to the gymnasium in school when his name was called. He was instantly intimidated by the hanging bed sheets which made a simple cubicle for privacy. But the sheets also gave an eerie, ghostly look of Halloween shrouds around the makeshift clinic. The elderly gentleman who received Harry wore a white jacket with a stethoscope dangling from his neck. He had a kind, reassuring smile. The other man was much younger and had a large notebook in which he hastily jotted notations after asking a few questions.

"Come, come," said the young, sallow-faced man behind the thick-lensed glasses. "We don't have all day. Unbutton your shirt."

Harry looked a little confused until the doctor said, in a kindly voice, "How are you, young man? I just want to listen to your breathing." It was Harry's first such examination he could remember but he understood quickly enough. He took deep breaths, his temperature was taken and then his pulse. He coughed, said "Ahhh" with wide open mouth when asked, and let the doctor do the chest thumping. He stood up on his toes when asked, his tonsils were checked and he was breathing more easily until the doctor asked the next question: "Will you please lower your trousers so I can check for hernia?" Harry stood still, trying to remember if he'd ever heard the word hernia before and he didn't know what it meant. But he understood the trouser-lowering part.

Harry didn't mind if his mother, father, or brother saw his naked nether parts. After all, his family had seen those when he was given a bath when he was younger or when he was ill or needed motherly nursing. But exposure of private body parts to strangers in a public school without the presence of parents outraged his sense of privacy, modesty, and propriety. Harry had been taught to shun indecency and lewdness. Sometimes it was difficult to tell the differences between them and this seemed to be one of those times. To betray those teachings now was to betray Momma and Poppa. Without his parents present, Harry was dubious about following instructions of the doctor. Something snapped inside him.

"Didn't you hear the doctor? Don't worry, we're not going to hurt you," the young man with the notebook and thick glasses said to Harry. He might have been a learned man, but he had not yet learned enough to refrain from the arcane psychobabble with which he was about to impress the doctor while poor Harry trembled with fright. Harry felt the assurance given him was superfluous. He didn't answer. Instead, he gritted his teeth with anger.

"You miss your mommy, don't you?" the bespectacled one asked.

This is what caused Harry's loss of self–control. As if things were not bad enough, now his sainted mother had to be dragged into this "examination" by the psychologist, and Harry would allow no part of that. And there was something else he would not explain. The very thought of it caused him to bolt out of the makeshift examination room. He simply grabbed his shirt and jacket, spun around, charged through the bed–sheet curtains, and ran out.

"Do you see what I mean by the Oedipal complex that Freud is talking about?" the young assistant asked his older and wiser colleague.

"No, I don't," the doctor said with irritation.

"Did you not see that boy's defense mechanism as a part of his reaction formation?" the younger man insisted. "His superego denies what his id craves on a subconscious level. He is too young to understand but subconsciously he is sexually attracted to his mother at this age but doesn't know it. He is afraid his father will find out. He is at the right age when the sexual urge is finally making itself known through the subconscious. It's perfectly normal, you know. Do you see how our social values create psychic conflicts resulting in neurotic behavior? He is split between two opposing forces and this is the beginning of heboid schizophrenia."

The older colleague was dumbfounded by the pedantry. "You think you could tell all that from what you just witnessed in four minutes?" the doctor asked.

"Oh, there is much more to it that I could relate," the assistant said with an air of smugness, "but it's time for lunch in the cafeteria and it's on the house. Shall we go?" The doctor heaved a sigh of relief.

In the next two days an official form was mailed from the assistant's office to Harry's mother, whose presence was requested for the analysis of Harry's subconscious. The service was a new study and Harry's experience was the beginning of a new trend in sex education. The school psychologist had asked to speak first to Harry's brother, Garo, in an effort to ferret out a more enlightened understanding than he had hope of gaining from interviewing only Harry or his mother. Garo was mature for his age and also spoke much better English than his brother, so he might shed some light on the matter of Harry's curious behavior. He could also interpret more easily for their mother.

The idea was to help the assistant and his trainees, who were bound to need it at the forthcoming meeting. Garo arrived to face a school committee of two novice counselors and the psychologist. He was asked a few casual questions to put him at ease and then the committee got to the heart of the matter: What was Harry really like at home? How was he getting along with his mother? Why would he be so upset about a physical examination? and so on. The verbal fishing expedition was not getting anywhere until a team member told Garo about Harry's behavior during the physical exam session. One of the group asked Garo why his brother would even refuse to lower his trousers for a simple hernia examination, as all other boys had. Garo was taken aback and embarrassed by the question. How could he reveal such a thing about his brother, he asked himself, even if he knew? "Besides, it's none of your damned business," he thought to himself, and felt happy that his father was not there to ask for an explanation.

There was something going on here which seemed suspicious to Garo. He was frightened at the way a mountain was being made of a molehill. There was something he was not being told. Couldn't they see that his kid brother was ashamed of showing himself in such a disgraceful manner? This was simply not done among Armenians, at least. It was a cultural and ethnic taboo. Besides, how would these distinguished people feel if they were asked by strangers to drop their pants for public viewing of their private parts regardless of age? The psychologist got into the act, again.

"Are your mother and brother very close to each other?" he asked once more.

Garo thought to himself, "Are not all children close to their mothers?" Confused by such an odd question, he hesitated to respond. The psychologist pressed his question again about Harry's "closeness" to his mother and Garo answered that they were close. Then the psychologist asked why Harry had run out of the examination "room." Garo knew why his kid brother had dashed out of the gym because his brother had told him. Garo lost self–control. His face flushed with angry embarrassment. "Why? Garo blurted out. "Because my brother was ashamed of the printing on his shorts!" The pyschologist was stunned and his team was speechless.

"What printing, what are you talking about?" the psychologist incredulously asked Garo.

The kindly old doctor, who moments before had joined the group, said, "Son, we are trying to help you. Won't you go back to the beginning and tell us what this is all about?"
This reassured Garo a little and he went back to the beginning to overcome his own embarrassment. If they want to know, Garo said to himself, very well, tell them. His brother would forgive him.

"Our mother makes our underwear from flour sacks, which have printing on them," he stammered. "Sometimes, all the letters don't completely bleach out in the wash. This time, the letters *K* and *thur* washed out but the *ing* and *Ar* did not. Harry and I know the letters spell, 'King Arthur', *the* brand name of the flour printed on the sacks. We laughed because during the sewing Momma did not know she had set King Arthur upside down on his head instead of his behind. My brother felt so ashamed to show his printed behind that nothing in the whole world would make him lower his trousers so he ran out. That's all."

By this time, the committee was laughing without restraint. Garo had not intended to sound funny but it was just the way it came out. He could not fight back the tears which ran down his face because in a way he had betrayed his brother under the goading of that "brain doctor." The real doctor thanked Garo, tried to soothe his feelings, and walked him to the door. He said, "Tell your mother she needs not come in with your brother. We understand the problem."

The doctor returned to the conference room. The laughter had ceased but there was a silence at the way things had turned out and the psychologist was visibly disturbed. He felt utterly foolish at the way he had theorized to the doctor about the Oedipus complex.

"I am cancelling Mrs. Stepanian's appointment," the doctor reported to the group.

The psychologist instantly leaped to his feet and began to protest but the doctor looked at him sharply, waved him down and calmly said to him, "The source of your problem is not the Oedipus complex, whatever that is. It is King Arthur, the flour bags, and the way they were sewn together." The kindly doctor waved his hand for silence and exclaimed in a loud voice, "Long live King Arthur!" The group broke into laughter and responded, "Long live the King!" The good doctor waved his hand forward, inviting the group to follow for lunch.

Chapter 6
A Very Merry Christmas

Garo did not say anything to his parents but told his brother that he had written a letter to Santa Claus, asking for a Christmas package. He had heard some of the neighborhood kids talking about how they had sent letters to Santa, addressed to the Outlet Department Store, the largest store of its kind in Providence. Santa's address had been advertised in the local newspaper, he explained to Harry. Garo was sure nothing would come of it, since he'd always understood that Santa lived at the North Pole—but it did.

The truck arrived just before dinner. There was a knock on the door. Mariam said, "Come in," as she opened the door and two Boy Scouts in uniform entered with smiles and asked if the Stepanians lived there and she answered, "Yes," and added, in Armenian, "Merry Christmas!" The Boy Scouts handed a good-sized box to Garo who was seated nearest to the door, cheerfully wished the family a Merry Christmas and left. It was that simple, but one of the happiest surprises the brothers had ever received, a box filled with a few toys, candies, crayons, and other goodies. Without the generosity of Santa from the Outlet Department Store, there would have been no gifts for Garo and Harry from their parents this year—Dickron's income barely covered the meager essentials.

The Stepanian boys were agog with impatience throughout the following week. They knew that they were going to Boston with their parents in Uncle Hovsep's automobile, which was a new Ford. Few autos in the early 1930s were owned by Armenians of the immigrant community and the trip to Boston was an exciting adventure which required more than an hour to get there if no flat tires occurred en route. Flat tires were fairly

41

Douglas Avenue

routine but there were none this trip and by early evening they drove through the outskirts of the metropolis. They were in a section of town which was still illuminated by gaslight.

Uncle Hovsep drove carefully. It was already dark and the street lights were being lit by the lamp lighters, carrying their ladders. As Uncle drove slowly past, Garo peered through the back window, watching as one propped his ladder against the crossbar of a lamppost, made the short climb up, then flicked the flint tip of his lighter to the gas jet, turning on the light. In that part of the town few suspected that electricity would soon spoil the charm of yesteryear.

Garo was hypnotized by the silver–dollar–sized snowflakes as they floated downward, making him feel as if he were lifted upward and he strained to see where they got started. It was one of the loveliest sights Garo was to remember, a scene indelibly engraved in his mind, appearing by magic every time he experienced the first snowfall of winter, wherever he might be. Harry, the younger brother, was sound asleep with his head resting on his brother's shoulder.

Soon, they reached their destination. Garo and Harry rushed into Auntie's arms, then pummeled their cousins' shoulders, they were so glad to see each other. Uncle Hovsep's house always seemed like a castle with its fine furnishings and large rooms and all the toys the cousins had. The most exciting thing was to see Grandpa and Grandma, who had newly arrived from Constantinople in the old country, years after they had survived the genocide by some miracle.

When things calmed down Uncle Hovsep held a meeting. He had the boys come into the living room where the Christmas tree had already been set up. One at a time, each boy approached and sat next to him while Uncle Hovsep asked him what he wanted Santa Claus to bring him for Christmas. The house was filled with merriment for young and old alike.

Three days later, the Christmas tree's stand was covered with brightly colored gift packages to be opened soon. In the meantime the kids played games or dressed warmly to go outdoors and have snowball fights. The parents were visited by countrymen they hadn't seen in years.

The children were sleeping when Santa Claus must have come down the chimney to leave all the gifts under the tree.

They had meant to stay awake until his arrival, but somehow, he appeared only when they could no longer keep their eyes open and had fallen asleep—the cousins planned to keep a lookout for him again next year.

Arising early the next morning, in no time at all, everyone ate a quick breakfast, then waited in eager anticipation for Uncle to read names and distribute the presents Santa had supposedly sneaked down the chimney and placed around the tree. Garo could not believe it. He had told Uncle that no one could get him what he really wanted—a microscope. When he opened his gift, there it was! It may have been only a small toy one, but it was the most precious thing ever presented to him.

Although Auntie's house seemed like a palace to the children, it was nevertheless a feat to create sleeping arrangements for so many people. Garo and Harry made their bed on the couch in the living room, placing their pillows against opposite armrests. Providing some privacy, heavy velvet draperies between the living room and dining room were drawn together at night when Grandpa and Grandma retired. They slept in a folding bed, pulling it down and out each evening, from its wall enclosure in the dining room. Sometimes, the draperies were left open just enough so the boys could crane their necks and watch Grandpa and Grandma kneeling in prayer. The boys waited patiently until Grandpa finished his prayer always with the same ending: "Please, Almighty God, let us awaken in the morning. I vow that I will not drink any more whiskey or smoke any more cigarettes or shout at my beloved wife when she makes me angry. Amen."

When he awoke, he always told Grandma, "If you are awake please get my shot of whiskey and cigarettes as soon as you give yourself your diabetic injection."

When she had taken care of herself she attended to Grandpa's whiskey, just one shot, helped him get dressed and placed the cigarette box on its stand and led him to the table. As soon as breakfast was finished he asked the boys to help fasten his waistband, or cumberbomb as the boys called it. He downed his whiskey with a grunt of approval and secured one end of his cummerbund against the waist of his trousers. Grandpa held up the other end of the twelve-foot length of red sash as he asked whose turn it was to start rolling it around his waist.

Grandpa stood still, counting the number of wraps, while the boys took turns walking around him, pulling the fabric firmly about his middle. On occasion, he would growl, "That's too tight" or "That's too loose." Once in place, the old–fashioned waistband nicely kept his trousers up and his belly warm.

Next, Grandpa asked whose turn it was to roll the cigarettes. "And don't lie about how many you roll," he always admonished the boys. They took turns tapping the ends of the rolled, tobacco–filled thin tissue papers to distribute the tobacco evenly and then handed each one to Grandpa. He licked the paper's edge before tamping it in place, so that the wet edge of the paper would seal itself around the rolled–up tobacco. He did it expertly and perfectly. After all, the boxed tobacco was imported from the old country and cost a small fortune, which Uncle always paid. Sitting nearby, Grandma did not utter a single word because it was considered bad manners for a wife to speak without her husband's signaled approval in the presence of others.

On Christmas day, Grandma and her daughters set the table with Auntie's best china, silverware, and embroidered napkins and set out serving dishes and plates, creating a sumptuous table to behold. The turkey and ham were joined by Armenian delicacies—Armenian pickled grape leaves wrapped around ground and spiced meat (or sarmas), rice pilaf, homemade bread, green string beans cooked with finely chopped lamb, onions, and stewed with tomatoes in olive oil. Dessert followed with *pakhlava* pastry, and Armenian coffee Middle Eastern style, pistachio nuts, a sesame confection known as *halvah,* fruits and sugared watermelon–rind preserves topping it all off. No one could forget a dinner like that. Even Grandma cheated a little once a year at Christmas.

Grandma routinely sterilized her own hypodermic needles and syringe and each day she injected her diabetes into submission. Then, loaded with insulin, she always asked the other women if she would be all right later. Everyone agreed that she would be, of course, and this evening it couldn't hurt if she disregarded her rigid diet, so long as she didn't overdo it with the pakhlava.

Dinner was not quite finished when the doorbell rang and Auntie went to answer it and there stood her older brother,

Haig, and his wife! They had driven for many hours, through a heavy snowfall, in an automobile that malfunctioned half of the time. How delightful it was for family to be together.

When dinner was finally finished the adults started one of their interminable card games and the boys sneaked downstairs to the cellar. Harry disappeared under the stairs and hauled out several short lengths of wood and fed the smoldering fire in the furnace. In a short time, the wood quickly burned to coals and the boys pulled out a large bag of chestnuts and scattered some of them over the layer of coals. Once the chestnuts popped open, the boys pulled them out with a small shovel. After the remainder of the chestnuts had also been roasted, and shelled, the boys devoured them with smacking lips. It was a treat they had waited to enjoy again since last Christmas.

On the following afternoon, Garo and Harry witnessed a curious episode. Grandpa ordered Grandma to fetch his overshoes, hat, and coat. Donning his outdoor wear, he explained that he was going to the club to play backgammon with the old–timers. As soon as he left, Grandma hurried over to the living room window and gently drew the draperies back just enough to get a good peek. Auntie and her sister stood aghast. "Mother, what are you doing?" they asked in unison, refusing to believe what they were seeing.

Grandma answered, "I'm watching to see where he's really going and I'll wager it's to the market where he can stand inside the doorway. He just wants to watch those young women walk past on the outside, with their flouncing boobs and..."

"Mother, how can you say such a thing about Father! The Turkish government may have destroyed all vital records, but you know full well he's over 70 years old, for heaven's sake! At his age, how can Father be guilty of what you imply? Besides, everyone is bundled up in heavy overcoats. What could he possibly see?" the older sister asked, in disbelief.

"You just proved my point," Grandma retorted. "That's because you don't know your father like I do!"

Both sisters looked at each other and escaped to the kitchen where they lost control over their repressed laughter.

Four days later, all too soon, it was time for everyone to depart for home. They said farewell, having a good cry as they embraced one another in tears. Uncle drove Dickron and his family back to Providence.

Having arrived home to a cold house, the boys helped their father bring in the wood and start the fire in the stove. "I already miss the steam heat in Auntie's home," Harry complained.

"Poppa," Garo asked at dinner, "do you think we can have a nicer home one of these days?" Dickron bowed his head but did not answer. Mariam secretly pressed Garo's knee under the table, an unspoken request for discreet silence as she deftly changed the topic of conversation.

Chapter 7
Chestnut Trophies

Several boys had gathered around the horse fountain and were having a heated conversation about horse chestnuts. Harry insisted that they were ready for playing the game of "chesties" but the others disagreed, arguing that they were not yet ripe enough to play the game, but Harry won out. "Okay, fellers," he said, "I'm going by myself. See you later."

"For Pete's sake," Munjee shot back, "can't you wait a minute so I can go with you?"

"Yeah, me too," added Croakie, stepping out front. The others relented and followed his example.

The boys set off on more than a two–mile walk to the East Side Park which was on the other side of the State House. That's where the rich people lived. As they approached the high brick wall Harry threw up his hands signaling for silence. They were too close to risk being overheard. A few paces later the gang broke up and the boys walked single file until each chose a tree of his own to climb. It was not difficult, as the elm trees, in full foliage, provided more than enough coverage to hide the boys.

They held the outer layer of the horse chestnut gingerly to prevent puncture from stray thorns and then twisted them free from the branches. When enough of them fell softly on the grass below they were gathered and stuffed into pockets or gunnysacks. The gang regrouped to sit in a circle on the grass and watched Harry to make sure that he made no mistakes in equitably tossing out chestnuts to each of them until the dispensation was completed.

The boys then stropped their knives and gently peeled the outer shells away and refilled the sacks with the cleaned goodies. Swinging the sacks of shelled chestnuts over their shoulders, they headed for Harry's backyard.

Once there, they emptied their sacks. Harry produced a hand-

47

ful of nails and some of the other fellows supplied a number of old shoelaces. Using a chunk of wood as a hammer, Croakie drove one of the nails through a chestnut. Once the nail was pulled through it a hole had been created through which a shoelace was threaded. Finally, Croakie knotted one end of the shoelace. When he yanked the other end of the shoelace, the knot was pulled flush to the side of the chestnut.

Munchie, Harry, and the other boys followed suit, so that now each boy held a shoelace from which dangled a chestnut. The object of the game was to mightily swing a chestnut against the one being held up by the other player until one or the other's chestnut was cracked open and it fell from the shoelace.

One knew he had missed his mark especially if an opponent uttered a loud screech of pain followed by a vigorous finger and hand waving to shake off the sharp paralyzing pain. It was then that recriminations followed, one blaming the other for deliberate savagery. It didn't help too much in soothing the pain but it did resolve the victim to get even when it was his turn to retaliate.

"Let the fight begin!" Munchie gleefully sang out. Croakie obliged him by vigorously swinging his chestnut at Munchie's.

"Owee!" shouted Munchie, as the chestnut slammed into his knuckles. "You did that on purpose!" he accused Croakie with some profanity thrown in.

"Aw, come on, Munchie. You know how easy it is to miss the mark," Harry interjected. "You've got to move faster."

"Yeah, wait until he gets his when it's my turn to whack him." Munchie's fist had already begun to swell and was turning a sickly black and blue.

Harry had the next shot. He swung hard at Croakie's dangling chestnut but Croakie jerked his hand the slightest bit, his chestnut sweeping to the side so that Harry's mighty swing missed it by just a hair.

As the boys took turns attempting to break one another's chestnuts, an agonizing cry was often let loose from another victim of a stray blow to the hand or fingers. So the games continued until the pile of chestnuts had been depleted and one player remained whose chestnut had survived to the end. He carefully wrapped his chestnut to add to his collection of trophies from previous victories.

Chapter 8
On the Count of Three

On a hot and humid July afternoon, Garo and Harry were sitting on a granite curbstone waiting to hear and feel the rumbling trolley car tracks from a distance. They had carefully placed the front end of a six–inch spike on the track when Harry said, "I think it's coming now," and both boys lifted their heads to see if the pulley, connected by a long mast to the trolley, was riding along the overhead electric cable. The blue crackling sparks when the pulley hit the interconnecting linkage was followed by the clanking of the trolley's iron wheels on the track, and then the thump–thump of the wheels as they flattened the tip of the spike. The trolley sped on.

If done correctly, the result was a nail with an inch or so of the tip ovately swaged. The flattened edges could then be filed to a razor sharpness. With a wooden handle attached, it made a neat carving tool for miniature work. It was a trick that Garo, the inventor of the technique, told only a very few friends, after swearing them to secrecy.

The Stepanian boys were admiring their work when they heard the voice of Mr. Mellone from a block away. "Wartee malone, ripe tomeetoes, and pie eatin' appoles," his voice sang out. He would raise his reins and bring them down sharply with a snap so his horse would not slacken his pace. The pulled wagon was loaded with fruit and vegetables. Every so often Mr. Mellone would stop the wagon so homemakers, standing by, could critically examine which produce looked good for the evening meal.

Mr. Mellone was careful when doing this because some of the neighborhood kids would sneak behind the wagon and swipe a peach or apple and run away before the vendor could see them. If he saw the thieves in time, his favorite ploy was to yell, "The goyn, give me the goyn" in his Yiddish accent, and reach over to his seat pretending to fumble for an imaginary gun for protection. But the kids knew when he was bluffing. After scaring them off, he would chuckle at the success of his bluff because the mothers of these boys were his best customers. It was they who bought most of the eggplants when the rest of his customers didn't know what an eggplant was. So, he would add a few pennies to the sale price of produce they purchased later, passing on the cost of his loss due to theft.

On this day his poor tired horse had picked up his gait because he was approaching the water fountain which the city had long ago placed on the corner of Douglas and Chalkstone Avenues. The iron fountain was about four or five feet tall by three feet or so in diameter and an easy reach for a horse. It must have weighed what looked like a ton, containing the cold water which gently overflowed the top. No one knew what turned the water on and off. One of the most intriguing sights was to see those poor panting creatures gulping water on a hot summer's afternoon. On occasion, even the kids drank from it or soaked their heads on the blistering hot summer days.

Nearing the fountain, Mr. Mellone tugged on the reins to slow his critter down. He had a firsthand view of what was coming and it came loaded. With uplifted tail, as he hurried along, the horse exploded a few loud blasts of intestinal gas, announcing the arrival of ploppings for several paces. The odds may have been astronomical but the bulk of the matter landed right in the middle of the street directly across from Barron Boghos's gate. In fact, the old man had heard the wagon's rumbling approach and waited to see if his hunch would pay off and it had, indeed. His hoped-for treasure lay there, in a steaming pile, so he called out for his grandson, who was nearby, commanding him to go back to his yard and get the pail and shovel. The Barron wanted Mother Nature's bountiful blessings for his garden fertilizer, which did a better job than commercial varieties.

Garo looked at the steaming pile in the middle of the street and knew there was no way to recover it before the grandson returned. The boys saw the answer to the problem simultaneously.

There was a long shallow cardboard box, of the standard

type for delivery of sliced American sandwich bread to the grocers of the *odar* or non–Armenian neighborhood, which lay crushed and pushed against the curbstone. The box had been squashed and dirtied with mud from bypassing motor vehicles. When the boys looked each other in the eye, they knew exactly what to do and they moved like lightning. They pulled the box away from the curb, tore it apart and grabbing a corner each of the large middle section, pushed it together in a rough version of a scoop. They ran to the treasured pile and with perfect unison shoveled up their prize, then ran down the street dodging the vehicular traffic.

When they got far enough away, Garo shouted, "On the count of three, let 'er go." They swung the makeshift carrier to and fro, counting, "one, two, three" and slung the still steamy cargo across the street. Garo and Harry stood there laughing uproariously.

"Come and get it!" Harry shouted with a sing–song crescendo. "I wonder what that skinflint will tell Poppa about us, now," Harry said.

"He won't say anything," Garo responded. "He's too afraid of being laughed at if the neighbors find out."

"How will neighbors find out?" Harry wondered aloud.

"Because we will start the rumors," Garo snickered.

They knew that Barron Boghos would never go to their father complaining about what they had done because it was too embarrassing for an old man to care about what others might think of him for getting hysterical about—manure? Who could possibly say that Barron Boghos did not deserve this?

By the time the poor grandson came out with the pail and shovel, it was much too late. Barron Boghos was so livid with rage and embarrassment that he dealt his poor grandson a heavy slap on the cheek.

The Stepanian boys flinched as though they had also been struck and they hurt with indignation for the little boy. "That kid, Varky, is a good playmate of ours. I feel like we got him into trouble," said Garo.

"We didn't mean to. We were only having fun," protested Harry, frowning with worry.

"That's true," Garo acknowledged.

"Maybe we could treat him to an ice cream cone when the ice cream truck comes through," suggested Harry, hopefully.

"Yeah, that would make it up to the kid, but where do we get the dough to pay for it?" responded Garo. "Two scoops cost a nickel—that would be fifteen cents for the three of us," he reminded Harry.

Feeling foolish because he knew how tough it was to put together enough pennies to buy just one cone, Harry reconsidered his suggestion. After a moment's hesitation, however, he exclaimed, "I have it! The ice cream man sells waffles for two cents a piece—we could afford to buy two for us." Although ice cream was better, waffles were good, too, and Harry could already taste the light–as–air waffle, drenched in syrup.

"That's a good idea. We'll buy a cone just for the kid," agreed Garo.

"The other day, Moushy wanted to buy a wooden knife I carved—I could ask him for nine cents and we'd be in business," said Garo. "I'll ask him if he's still interested."

Later in the week, having sold his knife to Moushy, Garo and Harry went looking for Barron Boghos' grandson, Varky. They found him playing by himself in his backyard. "Hi, kid," Garo called out to the boy.

Varky looked up from his solitary game of marbles, and recognizing Garo and Harry and recalling their recent prank which had cost him dearly, he responded warily with a hesitant "Hi."

"We're sorry for what happened the other day," Harry blurted, "and we'd like to make it up to you."

"How about it, kid?" Garo asked. The kid was immediately on guard.

"Why do ya wanna do that for me?" the kid asked, dumbfounded.

"Can't we do you a favor without you gettin' suspicious?" Suspicion on the boy's face was replaced by a look of disbelief, then one of eagerness, as he answered, "Okay."

"We're spendin' more on you than on ourselves. You just can't believe us, can you," Garo said with a laugh. Then they all laughed and Varky laughed the hardest, knowing that his chums had hit on a secret truth.

"That's settled then. Follow us," said Garo and the three boys took off for the spot on their street where the ice cream truck was expected to arrive shortly.

The merry tune broadcast by the ice cream truck was heard long before it appeared, rounding the corner onto Douglas

Avenue. A small group of boys and girls was already waiting impatiently to order their treats.

Coming to a stop, the cheerful vendor opened his window for business. "Who's first?" he asked, smiling to the group already gathering around.

"I am!" asserted a little girl.

"What'll you have?" the vendor asked her. He offered an assortment of candy toppings for the cones, chocolate sprinkles, peppermint pastels, and others, which the girl critically considered before making her choice.

Garo, Harry, and Varky were next in line. "We'll take two waffles and a cone," said Garo. He turned to Varky, asking, "What flavor do ya want?"

"Chocolate," Varky said, not believing the ice cream cone was really his until Garo paid the vendor.

Once the transaction was complete, the boys retreated to the side of the road where they immediately began to munch their goodies. Garo looked up to see tears running down Varky's face. "What's the matter?" Garo asked.

"Nuthin'," Varky mumbled self–consciously.

"Then why are you cryin'?" Garo asked.

"Because no one but family ever treated me to an ice cream before," he answered softly.

Chapter 9
Leonard's Pond

Leonard's Pond was well known to the many kids from Douglas Avenue. It was more like a river and flowed swiftly over the high dam which was about ten or fifteen feet high. On the shallow side of the dam was what passed for a beach. It was everyone's favorite swimming hole. Some of the more daring souls would dive off the high dam, which had become the test for bravery because below it the water churned white with foam. Previous dives had given Garo a personal sense of the danger.

On a hot sunny day the gang went there, changed into their bathing suits and three or four of the boys stood on the edge of the dam gazing at the water, daring each other to go first. From where they stood they could see what looked like a steel bucket, floating upright, while bobbing and swirling crazily in the turbulent water. The best guess was that it was too far away to be taken seriously as a hazard.

The boys noticed about an eight-foot length of diving board someone had fastened to the top edge of the high dam. Garo walked the length of it, bounced on it a few times and decided it had a nice spring to it. He took a final bounce hard on its end—it hurled him higher and farther out than he had imagined. The kids, who were watching from the bank, let out a horrified groan. They feared that Garo had not estimated his clearance accurately. He soared through the air with too much power and distance.

He came down gracefully enough but his outstretched hands cleaved the water, barely missing the floating edge of the steel bucket bobbing in the swirling water. He was surprised at how badly he had misjudged it when the roiling water slammed the bucket against the side of his leg. He knew that if he had struck its rim his skull would have been split like a watermelon. He was shaking when he emerged from the churning water. Garo returned to the submerged edge of the beam that formed the top surface of the waterfall, removed the diving board and flung it over the top. He would never forget his close call. A few days later, in an uncanny flashback, Garo would recall his nearly disastrous dive. It was to become a permanent part of his memory to haunt him several times during the rest of his life.

One afternoon, five or six of the boys went to the movies to see an "action" picture, so called by the kids, about divers on a sunken ship. That's when Garo got the idea. He was fascinated by the old-fashioned diving suits and helmets with air bubbles gurgling up while two divers were locked in a dagger fight, each trying to slash the oxygen pipe of the other. It didn't take long for Garo to decide that he had to have a diving suit and get a real look at what was at the bottom of the murky water in Leonard's Pond. He wished there would be a lurking octopus there as he had seen in the movie, although he laughed at his own doubts about it.

Leaving the movie theater, Garo asked his brother, "Harry, do you want to help me make a diving suit?"

"What do you mean by making a diving suit?" Harry responded incredulously. "How do we do that?"

"I have a plan, but first we need to raise some money." Garo answered.

Garo and Harry spent several days carefully scouting the neighborhood. The city was upgrading a couple sections of overhead high-voltage wiring which had long since worn out its usefulness. A lot of discarded wire had been cleared away and the boys got to it just in time to carry off all they could retrieve before the big removal truck showed up. They then burned all insulation off the wires, pounded them into smaller compact masses and sold them at Abes's junkyard. Copper wire in those days sold for two cents a pound but Abe would pay no more than a penny a pound. He's a crook, Garo thought, but all the kids knew that. There was nothing to be done about the outrage. Garo gave in. Now, at least, he and Harry had some cash to buy a waterproof glue with which he planned to patch together the diving suit.

Garo owned an old poncho, made of an artificial, rubberized material, which was popular for boys' wear but not very durable. His had been accidentally torn at the hem, and was hanging around in the cellar somewhere. He and Harry could fashion the "diving suit" from the remains, he thought.

Harry asked impatiently, "How do we make the helmet?"

"That's easy," Garo said, "Let's go to the dump. We need an olive oil can."

Five–gallon olive oil cans were easy to find since the Armenian women used olive oil in large quantities instead of the salad oils which were considered as cheap *odar* or foreign substitutes. Tin snips easily cut a square hole out of one side of the can and a piece of glass with a wooden frame was fastened into the opening. The top of the can was fitted with a garden hose coupling to which the hose would be attached.

It took a couple weeks of hard work to get everything hooked up together. Unknown to the brothers, however, their mother had occasionally removed the tarp under which the apparatus was hidden. She knew nothing about diving suits but as it neared completion she could not believe what she saw. A strange feeling came over her that something terrible was about to happen. She told the boys' father about it and suggested he should check the backyard. Dickron did, but it rang no bells for him.

Dickron had a close friend who worked in the foundry in the sandblasting shop. He wore a leather suit and a helmet, and breathed forced air and oxygen when the blaster was on. The blaster, under enormous pressure, spewed out sand against iron parts and fittings to clean them of rust and debris. At his friend's invitation, Dickron watched him from a distance to see how it worked and he could see at a glance that by adjusting the nozzle the blast of sand could easily kill a man. But what provided the critical insight was the helmet, which meant the difference between life and death, and the helmet and air hose told him all he wanted to know about what his sons were up to.

Prepared for their first test dive, the brothers stacked their diving gear on the wagon used for moving garden soil, and hauled the load to the pond.

Garo donned the rubberized diving suit, then after some

minor adjustments, Harry helped fit the helmet over Garo's head. Harry signaled that he would blow air through the attached hose to check it out.

The minute Harry's spent breath reached Garo's lungs, Garo gagged and choked on the stale, tainted air and frantically struggled to yank the helmet off. He was still gagging and gasping when Harry got him clear of the helmet. "You want to try again to be sure?" he asked, knowing that Garo would not call his bluff. He was still trying to find his breath. Harry turned blue trying to hide his laughter.

They tried again. Garo entered the water and submerged himself with only the end of his breathing tube remaining above the surface. Not knowing his elementary physics, Garo thought that because he'd bound the hem of his "suit" around his middle it would keep most of the water from filling up in his helmet but the water seeped into the helmet from the neck fitting. Garo realized a tighter fitting would have to be constructed and a tire pump would have to be fitted to the hose, but everything else seemed to be all right. Encouraged by early indications of success, the boys hauled the gear home to make adjustments. They slept soundly expecting the next dive to take place in a couple of days.

The following day was Sunday and all the hardware stores were closed. It was irksome to wait until Monday when the boys could buy the needed parts. To spend their idle time to good end, they went to see the new Western at the "scratch house." That same day, a gang of kids went swimming at the beach near the upper end of the high dam. Midget, about five years old, accompanied the group with his older brother. It was late in the afternoon when Midget's brother noticed his absence and gave the alarm. The boys searched frantically. Not finding Midget, the brother ran home to tell his mother that he was missing. In a few moments, half the neighborhood had run to the pond. A fire truck and the police wagon arrived with a professional diver who quickly got into his diving gear and disappeared into the dark, murky depths of the pond.

The rescue team reasoned that the swift current would have swept any movable body down against the base of the dam above which was iron grating to prevent anything from floating through. It didn't take long for the diver, with a tug on his line, to signal the crew above. Soon, the diver reappeared from the depths of the water, carrying the limp body of poor Midget. Most who recognized him stood in silence, but his father broke down in tears and sobbed with heartrending cries of, "My son, my son!" and looking to the heavens, "Why, why?"

Poor Midget. What a tragic end to a young and beautiful life. No one in the gang with whom Midget had gone swimming could say what might have happened. No one remembered seeing him. There were ugly rumors that some of the older kids had thrown Midget into the water to teach him to swim. But the police had turned up no evidence after much questioning.

The day following Midget's drowning, Garo and Harry were downtown looking for the parts they needed to make improvements to their diving suit. Returning home with their purchases, they were stunned at the sight which greeted their eyes. The tarp covering their diving apparatus had been yanked to the side, the helmet had been smashed to a pulp, the diving suit had been slashed into pieces and the rest of the equipment had been destroyed, one way or another.

Who could have done such a thing? Shaken, the boys went to Momma to find out. She refused to answer questions. All she said was, "Ask your father when he gets home."

And when Poppa got home he admitted he had committed the deed. He let the boys know he was angry and roundly chastised them. He said he knew all about what the boys had been up to. When the boys remonstrated, his anger suddenly exploded. The boys had rarely seen him so angry and they didn't understand why he was now. "You want to know why I'm, angry don't you?" he shouted at the boys. Both of his sons fearfully nodded their heads in assent.

Poppa asked, "Midget was your friend, wasn't he? But he's dead! He drowned yesterday where you go swimming. Many times your mother and I have told you not to go swimming at Lennitz Pound," he said, pronouncing the English name for the pond the way it sounded to him. "What would we have done if it had been you? Do you know what Midget's parents are going through now?"

He sobbed just after his last question and turned away so as not to be seen by his sons as he broke down. He couldn't go on anymore so he walked away in a daze at his own behavior.

His sons didn't seem to realize that they might drown just as Midget had if they were to dive in their fabricated suit.

The boys walked to the baseball park and soon the gang showed up. It seemed odd but they really didn't want to play ball. Instead, they all told about how their parents had often scolded them for swimming at Leonard's Pond to avoid such a tragedy. They had made their sons promise never to go to the pond again. The sons promised because all of them felt some guilt for not having kept a lookout for Midget.

In about two weeks the guilt wore off. One by one, the boys went swimming again. Every one of them was positive that Midget would understand.

In retrospect, Garo felt that the events of that summer were linked together in an uncanny way that could not be dismissed as pure coincidence: first, there was his near–fatal dive from the dam; next, the movie he and Harry had seen with its thrilling underwater sequences; then there was all their work that went into making the diving suit; followed by Momma's strange, mysterious feelings about the goings–on in the backyard; and last but not least, there was the tragedy of Midget's untimely death, and Poppa's response to it by suggesting that he and Harry could also drown. Taken together, these incidents formed a pattern which created a meaning for Garo's memory bank with Midget's death. Death took on a personalized meaning connected to Garo through Midget. The word death became something real, with substance. Garo would think of how precarious life was, anytime something reminded him of the fate which had claimed Midget's life.

Chapter 10
Foul Ball

Harry was playing in his front yard when he heard someone calling his name. He looked up to see Viken waving at him. Viken was from New York and once a year about this time, he showed up for his vacation with his cousins who lived across the street from the Stepanians. The boys were close friends and ran to greet each other with a warm embrace. Shortly thereafter, several of the gang showed up and it was time to head for the park and play another game of baseball.

It was Harry's turn at bat and he connected with a good one. He was sliding into second base just as he was tagged. An argument broke out about whether he was safe or not. "You f...ing hoover!" someone yelled. "He was safe by a quarter mile."

Viken broke out in laughter. When someone asked him what was so funny he answered, "You guys from Providence always say 'hoover' instead of 'whore.' You never say it right."

The Stepanian boys were finishing dessert that evening when Harry said to his brother, "If what Viken says is true, then we've been saying it wrong for a long time. What was Viken talking about? Everyone always says 'f...ing hoover.'"

Poppa Stepanian had been listening to the boys on and off and when he thought he heard President Hoover called "that f.... Hoover," he exploded. "What did you call the president of our country? How can you degrade anyone with such a filthy word, especially our president? Do you know what it really means?"

Both boys were speechless for a moment. They weren't certain what *whore,* or *hoover* or the *f* word meant, only that these were "dirty" words—but they hadn't spoken ill of the President of the United States!

61

Garo protested, "Poppa, we would never swear in speaking of our president. Harry and I were discussing our baseball game this afternoon. One of the boys on our team was defending Harry against another boy who claimed Harry was out on second base. He was angry and shouted, 'You f...ing hoover' at the other player."

"Well, sons," said their father, "such language is not acceptable whether you're referring to a teammate or anyone else."

"Yes, Poppa," the boys dutifully replied.

Vigen's comment remained a mystery and all the kids continued to use the phrase and none of the Armenian kids knew what it really meant. And their parents took care not to explain its meaning for obvious reasons.

About two months later Garo was with a group of *odar* boys when their conversation drifted to an off-color topic. When one of the older boys used the word whore and Garo asked for a definition of the term, he was given a full explanation which developed into a sex lecture way ahead of its' time. He immediately realized that there were regional differences in pronunciation of the word whore and also that the Douglas Avenue boys were mistakenly pronouncing the Providence, Rhode Island version of it as hoover. What's more, he was mortified by what he heard about the sex act. He told Harry about it and they reached an agreement not to tell Poppa that they knew what they weren't supposed to know about presidential propriety, sex, linguistics, and parental secrecy.

"Don't you think we ought to tell Poppa that we know about it so he won't get mad at us for keeping a secret from him?" Harry asked, having second thoughts about his pact with Garo.

Garo insisted, "Oh no! That won't do and would only stir up more trouble. Do you swear you'll say nothing, cross your heart and hope to die if you do?" There was a prolonged silence and begrudgingly Harry finally agreed and made the sign of the cross to seal his promise.

After Viken had gone back to New York, the neighborhood boys continued to use the Rhode Island version of their favorite epithet. A habit of speech does not easily fall out of favor but also the boys feared that they might be suspected of showing off a sophistication which was phoney to them—if a hoover became a whore.

Chapter 11
A Disreputable Man

It had been a hard day looking for work and Dickron was especially tired when he finally joined his wife in bed that night. She had been reading and when she put her book down, she gave him a faint smile and said, "I'm so glad you have come to bed because I have something very important to tell you, if you're not too tired to listen."

He groaned a little and was barely awake enough to say, "Very well, say it now, dearest wife."

"I believe I'm pregnant," she said.

"What did you say?" he asked, sitting bolt upright as if someone had splashed him with a bucket of ice water.

"I said I think I'm pregnant," she repeated, softly.

"That's wonderful news," her husband declared joyfully, hugging her, "but why do you sound so sad?"

"Because you know that we cannot pay doctor bills," she replied anxiously.

"Dearest wife," he said, with a reassuring smile, "we have two fine sons and maybe this time we'll be blessed with a daughter. Please don't worry about it. We will figure a way out."

"I know we will, my dear man," she said and clenched her teeth so she would not have to ask, "How?"

Dickron slept fitfully but after breakfast he walked double-time across town for Dr. Kalian's office. There were no patients at this time of day so the good doctor took him in quickly and asked what the problem was. Dickron would rather have died than go into details, but he did.

"My wife feels that she is pregnant," he said with some hesitation.

"Well, that's not unusual, is it?" the kind doctor smiled, guessing what would come next and it did when Dickron said, "I don't know how I can pay for it now. I was laid off my regular job nearly two years ago because of this depression and have been working only part-time on any work I can find. And now this. I don't know what I'll do if something goes wrong. Can I pay you a little at a time as soon as I find a job? I don't know what else to do and I'm worried sick."

"Whoa, whoa," the doctor said. "Not so fast. Nothing will probably go wrong and we must believe that. Right now lots of married men have that apprehension. What kind of work did you do? If I remember correctly, you're a pretty good carpenter."

"I am, but who is building houses these days?"

"I'm not very good with a hammer," the doctor said, "and I can use a good carpenter for a small job. I need a fence built. Are you available for work soon?"

Dickron stopped breathing for a moment as his heart nearly pounded out of his rib cage. "When do you want me?" Dickron asked, eagerly.

"In a couple of weeks," the doctor said. He opened a desk drawer and reached for a business card and a few dollar bills, pushed them across the desktop and said, "This is an advance to help you out. Call me in a couple of weeks and come by our house to take measurements and make a list of materials you'll need to get started. But bring your wife here for an exam before then."

Dickron walked home and thought of the reputation Dr. Kalian enjoyed in his community. He was known as a kind and generous man with sympathy for his compatriots and what they had suffered to stay alive. Moreover, he delivered most of their babies.

Someone had once said that the doctor had a heart as big as a whale's. He had just proved it, Dickron thought to himself. He couldn't wait 'till he got home to tell his wife the good news.

He was up early the next day to find an interim job for a couple day's work, but without any luck. Just as he was crossing the street he saw Topalian, better known as Topal, coming toward him. "Oh, no," Dickron thought to himself. That was the last man he wanted to see. In fact, that was the last person most people—men or women—in the community would want to see.

He lived on the other end of town. His reputation as a disgrace to his community was well established. It was common knowledge he went on drinking sprees every few months. When he was drunk, his temper was vicious. Even though Topal was married to one of the finest and most gentle of women anywhere, he was always on the lookout for *odar* women of loose morals whenever he ventured outside the ethnic community. His wife was deathly afraid of him. Rumors had it that he beat her often. It was unthinkable behavior in the community, which avoided him like the plague.

Although childless in his present marriage, Topal had an older daughter by a previous marriage. His first wife had been killed during the Turkish genocide but their daughter had survived, and for a while, she had been taken care of as an orphan by an American relief society. Once it was discovered that her father was still alive, parent and child had been reunited in America. She was a young woman now, with an American education, unmarried, and so still living in her father's house.

Topal worked at Brown and Sharpe, an internationally famous industrial complex, which produced much of the world's precision tool instruments. He earned a decent living—he had some kind of connection with a middle-level manager who gave him special treatment.

When Dickron saw Topal coming at him, he nodded and stepped aside but it was too late by a few moments and that's when Topal grabbed him by the elbow and said "Hello, countryman. How are you?" in a loud, boisterous voice. Dickron, who never forgot his manners, returned the salutation. Topal started an amiable conversation and Dickron could not be rude so he resigned himself to listen. He became aware that Topal was nudging him closer to the doorway of the Ararat Restaurant a few steps away.

"Oh, here's the restaurant," he said as though he had just seen it. "Why don't we go in and let's have coffee on me, eh?" He ordered coffee and *simits*, an Armenian bread roll. Dickron was closely studying his host and could not believe that such a generous and gregarious man could be as bad as everyone on Douglas Avenue said he was. Their conversation was mundane and Topal asked how Dickron was coping with the Depression and Dickron went on the defensive again. "Well," he said, "it could be better of course, but we're doing well enough," and he blanched a bit at his own fabrication. Topal's eyes narrowed to slits as he guessed the truth and the embarrassment it caused the other man.

"You know," he said to Dickron, "I have influence with the management, so if you need help let me know and I'll see what I can do for you."

Rising from the table, Dickron said, "Thank you. You are kind indeed, but we're doing just fine." They parted company.

Dickron arrived home in a kind of daze and when he related the events at the doctor's office his wife's eyes moistened with tears. "God bless that man," she said.

"We can go to see him any day you say."

"Can we go by trolley car so I won't have to walk so far?"

"Of course," her husband answered, "but let me finish the story. The good doctor hired me to build his fence for him. And now I need you to help me. He wants me to check things out and make a list of what I think the job requires so he can call the list in for delivery to his home. Your writing is better than mine so I will tell you what I need in Armenian if you will write the words down and we can mail the list to the doctor's office to be translated into English. He can have it mailed to the company. Now for some other news."

"I'm sure you have heard of Mr. Topalian. He ran into me near the Ararat Restaurant and I couldn't get away. We had a talk which turned out to be a surprise. He said he would try to get me a permanent job if I wanted one at the factory. You know that I don't like him, but I didn't know what to say except that I would think it over. My surprise is that he would make such an offer to me. We hardly know each other. What do you think is going on?"

Mariam replied, "From what I've heard about him, I would say no, stay away from that man. He is a scary thing from all the rumors I've heard about him."

"Well, I've heard the same rumors, too. But I wonder if it's just spiteful talk. Anyhow, nothing came of it. I think he was in a talkative mood and I tried to be decent about it by hearing him out. That's all."

Later in the afternoon at dinner, he asked the boys how they felt about helping him in a few days when the lumber and materials arrived. The kids were thrilled because their father trusted them and asked for their help. Also, they would have a chance to learn something about building fences.

The doctor's office sent a message, soon enough, to say that the material Dickron had asked for had been delivered. He was tickled pink to go to the site with his sons pulling the red Flier Wagon, filled with his tool box and implements. He instructed the boys on what was to be done as they helped him drive a few stakes into the ground for alignment of the post holes. Then they began digging into the gravelly surface to get a start for the deeper holes. "Don't forget," he said, "the holes need to be three feet deep and about four feet apart."

At first, it was a lot of fun for the boys, who really worked hard, but soon enough they hit the rocky bottom. They took a break for lunch and went back to work, each on a separate hole. Three hours later the boys had slowed down appreciably and their father thought it wise to call it a day for their sake. When they reached home their aching muscles told them they had put in a fair day's work.

It took about two weeks, on and off, to dig the holes, set the posts, nail the pickets, and finally paint the completed fence. One of the *odar* neighbors stopped by and told Harry that he had misspelled the words on the sign propped next to the fence. It was not wet pant, but wet paint, he explained.

Garo was asked to telephone the doctor's office and advise him that the job was done. Dr. Kalian was pleased by the news and asked that Garo's father come over to the office tomorrow so that he could be paid the remainder of what he was owed.

When Dickron walked into the office, he exchanged greetings and smiled as he noted that the doctor's usually dignified appearance had changed somewhat. He was now wearing a smock and watering some plants in the window box. "Well," the doctor said, "I hope these plants grow this time because they failed miserably last year."

"What are they?" Dickron asked.

"They are supposed to produce cucumbers. My wife loves to pickle them," he said. "By the way, we approve of the way you put that fence up and think it's beautiful. How much more do I owe you?"

"Pay me whatever you think it's worth," said Dickron.

"No, you tell me what you want," said the doctor.

Dickron was embarrassed. This was the kindly old gentleman who had brought his children into this world and given Dickron and his family the medical attention they needed any time, at bargain prices. The doctor sensed the problem. He knew what Dickron was thinking in old-country terms. Back there, one paid off his debts with an act of generosity and everlasting gratitude—not money.

"What if I provide your wife with the medical care she will requre during her pregnancy and delivery, with the understanding that my fee will be substantially reduced? We can negotiate that later. In the meantime, we don't have to worry about money. Just think about kindness, fairness, and trust. You know—the way it used to be in the old country."

Dickron felt jubilant and yet guilty at the same time. He knew the doctor was being merciful. "You are more than kind. Thank you," he said, "and I'm sure you know that the last man who thought like that was nailed to a cross. Thank you," he repeated. No more words were needed. Dickron hurried home to share the good news with his wife.

The months flew by and the financial pressures eased up a bit as Dickron got two or three part-time jobs and kept the family going. Eight months had gone by and Mariam needed another regular examination. She was doing well, the doctor said.

After a fruitless day of job hunting, Dickron returned home and his wife informed him that Topal had stopped by and asked that she tell her husband to meet him at the Ararat Restaurant the following Sunday. Dickron believed it was only to pass the time of day and had no special desire to do so but decided he would meet with Topal, anyway.

Sunday afternoon, Dickron entered Ararat Restaurant, where Topal was already seated at one of five small tables crowding the front end of the restaurant. As soon as he got close to Topal it was obvious he had been drinking, as his alcoholic breath spread the message. They drank Armenian coffee and chatted a bit and then Topal announced, "I have some good news for you. I spoke to my friend, the boss, and based on what I said about you he wants to see you, so come ready to work. Congratulations," he added.

Dickron sat silently for a minute. "You're joking, aren't you?" he asked.

"I don't tell jokes at this time of day, but I know what you mean. See me at seven-thirty in the morning at the main gate and I'll introduce you to the foreman at his office and get you signed up." He handed over a crudely drawn map of how to get there and then said, "Someday, maybe you can do me a favor." Dickron, out of gratitude, already wanted to return the kindness for its own sake, the old–country way. Was Topal goading him into a business transaction, with the expectation of a payback instead of a gift of kindness? Dickron couldn't tell whether he was being told a truth or being taken for an old–country donkey ride. They chatted for a while and when they got up, Dickron noticed Topal sway, holding on to his chair for balance. It was not a good sign.

Monday morning Dickron met the foreman who seemed like a decent man although he didn't say much. After some hand motions depicting his task, the boss handed Dickron an iron founding and pressed a switch which started a large–sized grinding wheel. Dickron had experience in the use of grinding wheels, although nothing so large. The boss watched Dickron deftly turn the finding against the grinding wheel and said, "Okay, you will do nicely." Then they did a tour in and around various machinery, after which the boss demonstrated how to use the time clock. Dickron was shown the men's room with its showers and then the steel closet for storing work clothes. Next, calling Dickron's attention to a long line of heavy wooden boxes containing an endless array of heavy iron parts, the boss indicated that Dickron should help him carry them to a grinder. Assigned to run the machine, he set to work until the five o'clock whistle blew. The floor boss showed up to chat briefly and say that he was pleased with the work Dickron had done. As Dickron punched out on the time clock, he felt happy with his first day's work.

Topal walked to the gate with Dickron and told him that he and his wife were invited to his home Sunday afternoon for dinner. Before Dickron could finish apologizing for his refusal of the invitation because he, too, had guests coming, Topal said in a sharp commanding tone, "Well, get rid of them. This is me asking you. Don't refuse me!" and turned away, walking toward his car. There had been a harsh, grating, and angry sound to Topal's voice. Dickron didn't like it and for the first time he sensed something sinister in the man, but he couldn't identify it.

Dickron and Mariam found Topal's address after a long two–trolley–cars ride. After dinner, the men talked about the sad state of affairs of the nation's economy. The women talked about babies and Topal seemed hypnotized by their conversation whenever he could catch part of what was being discussed without seeming too inattentive to Dickron. At last it grew late enough to take leave but not before Dickron left a box of Cremo cigars, which he could not really afford, and Mariam offered Topal's wife a superb piece of her hand embroidery.

Topal and his wife accepted these gifts, but only after they and their guests observed the Armenian custom dictating that the donor insists several times that the recipient take his gift lest the donor be suspected of an empty gesture, and that the recipient refuses with equal vigor lest he be suspected of greed. After several offers and refusals, each gives in, feeling satisfied that he has averted any suspicion of being stingy or greedy.

A few weeks after Mariam's baby was born, Topal stopped by and began a chat with Dickron about the new baby's birth and when the lunch whistle sounded he motioned Dickron to follow him to the lunchroom where they sat down at the end table where they were fairly isolated. Topal seemed to want privacy. Both dug into their lunches packed by their wives.

Topal was eager to start the conversation with chitchat but suddenly shifted the topic. "How are your wife and baby doing?" he asked. Dickron was startled by his question since unless two friends are very close, they rarely ask each other about their wives' or children's affairs, which are respected as part of the woman's world. Topal warmed up to the topic and said, "I want to ask you a very important question. When you need help you know that I'll help you. Right? Now I need you to help me."

"Of course," Dickron said. "I will do anything that I can do to help you." Topal smiled. Dickron didn't like the look in his eyes.

"You know," Topal explained, "my wife and I have never been able to have a baby and she has been very unhappy over that after all these years. You have raised two fine boys.

We think that you will be glad to let us legally adopt your baby girl as our own. Of course we will wait until you talk this over with your wife, and we would pay for all expenses. Let us know as soon as you can, will you?"

Dickron sat stunned. In the old country such a demand would never have been made. It was disrespectful. In fact, it was insulting even in the way it was proposed. Such an expectation was unthinkable. It offended the sanctity of the family. Now Dickron began to understand what his relationship to Topal was all about.

After several moments of silence, Dickron answered slowly, breathing heavily, trying to stay calm. When he finally answered he said in a soft voice, "You are serious, aren't you? I don't need to ask her because I know what she will say, so let me say it for both of us, 'Go to hell!' How dare you ask me such an insulting question? Our baby is not for sale. You may ask me for anything I have except my children or my wife." He got up to leave and Topal saw the look in Dickron's eyes—a look he had never seen before. It occurred to him that perhaps Dickron was not as soft a pushover as he had first appeared.

A few weeks went by and then it happened. Dickron was carrying a heavy box of foundings when Topal abruptly turned a corner and ran into Dickron with just enough force to cause Dickron to lose his grip on the box. It slipped from Dickron's hands and he sidestepped but not quickly enough before one of the heavy foundings landed on his toe and caused enough pain to make his mother cry. Topal walked by, leaving Dickron alone to box the scattered foundings.

Dickron was astounded at what seemed like deliberate rudeness, added to injury, but he said nothing. Instead, after work, he waited by the gate until he saw Topal approaching and when he came close enough Dickron hobbled in front of him. "I think you dropped those foundings deliberately," he accused.

"What if I did?" Topal asked belligerently, provoking Dickron.

"Don't try it again," Dickron warned, "or it'll be the biggest mistake you ever made."

Something in his expression gave Topal a fleeting wave of fear. He had never seen Dickron so cold and threatening. He forced himself to laugh, hoping that it would cover up his real feelings. Then he stepped past Dickron and silently walked away. For the next few days Topal hated himself for having cowered before a man whom he thought was a timid soul. To think that he had helped Dickron to get his job! It tormented him and he had to find a way to salve his wounded feelings and get even. Meanwhile, Dickron went straight to the doctor, who splinted the broken toe.

A few days following his confrontation with Topal, Dickron left one evening to go to the club. The boys promised to stay at home with their mother and baby sister while he was gone.

That same evening, Topal had already drunk quite heavily after dinner when he made the decision to confront Dickron and his wife. He stumbled into his car and drove toward Douglas Avenue, making a left-hand turn on Derry Street, which was dark and deserted. Another left turn and he was on Douglas. He stopped, switched off his headlights and was now one house away from his destination.

Dickron had said to his wife that he would return in a couple of hours from the club, where he was going for the usual evening card game. As he left the house, his right-hand turn placed him a short walk from the club. Had he glanced in the opposite direction, he would have seen Topal's car parked behind him, beneath the dull illumination of a street light.

Topal noted Dickron's departure and waited until he disappeared from sight before clambering from the car. With Dickron's unexpected absence from home, Topal thought with satisfaction, his plan to claim the baby would be that much easier.

Mariam and her boys were startled when suddenly there was a loud hammering on the door, beyond which they heard Turkish profanity, uttered in a slurred voice. She knew instantly to whom the voice belonged. It was Topal's.

The pounding on the door increased and he shouted, "Open the door!" over and over again.

"What do you want? Go home," she replied. "Go home, and leave us alone!" By this time, she was genuinely afraid.

"What I want, eh? I tell you what I want. I wanna screw you. Then I wanna take your baby home to my wife, okay?" He laughed with one of the most evil laughs she'd ever heard.

Strangely, there was an eerie silence which followed. Topal had gone back to his car. He snatched a folded blanket from the back seat and haltingly returned to the house. In a few minutes his voice was heard again. It came from the kitchen side of the house. "The baby. I wanna the baby," he said in broken syllables. Mariam went to the window and raised the shade. In the dim light she saw Topal and beyond him, his parked car and she wondered how he had managed to drive it in his inebriated condition.

In the brief moments he had been to the car, Garo had stepped to the cabinet drawer in the kitchen and removed a long-bladed carving knife. "Give me that. I don't want you to hurt yourself," his mother said, but Garo whisked it away saying, "better I get hurt than you. Step back, Momma, please."

Close to the side of the house ran a low picket fence. Mariam watched with disbelief as Topal managed to climb to the top of it after losing his footing several times. Just as Topal started to stand up on the fence rail he slipped, swayed again and fell to the ground on the far side, landing with a thud. In his stupefied state he didn't seem to be hurt or stoppable. He got to his feet again and shinnied up the header to which the adjacent pickets had been nailed. This time he made it. He had wrapped and tied the blanket around his waist which he now undid. Mariam and Garo watched with apprehension as Topal wrapped the blanket around his arm and fist.

Somehow, Topal was precariously balancing himself on the top of the rail. "You open window!" he screamed at Mariam. In the next instant, Topal jumped to the ground beneath the kitchen window. He tried to force open the window but it was latched from the inside. "Are ya gonna open the window?" he shouted. No answer. In a maniacal fit of rage, he smashed his wrapped fist against the windowpane, shattering the glass. Then he began to curse in the foulest Turkish language.

He shrieked, "My wife wants your baby and I want to screw you. Do you understand me?"

Mariam had instinctively disliked Topal from the moment she had first seen him. There was something about the man which she found repulsive.

There are moments in life when one can change radically into the opposite of what one has been during a lifetime. Mariam, a sweet gentle lady, changed in a split second. She suddenly cried, "Yes, I understand you," grabbed her kitchen knife away from Garo, and screamed, "You crazy man, you lay one finger on my baby and I will kill you!" as her fingers tightened around the knife handle. For the first time in his life, Topal understood the fury of a mother whose child's life is in danger. Topal stayed his hands.

An automobile sped by and lit up the street for just a few seconds, but it was enough for Garo to see the unmistakable figure of his father coming toward them. *Thank God Poppa was home early!* Garo shouted at the top of his voice, "Hurry, Poppa, hurry, we are in danger with a drunken Mr. Topal!" Then Mariam and Harry started to yell. Dickron did not hear all their words but he knew that something was radically wrong.

Nearby, a shadowy figure hurriedly opened the door of a parked car, climbed inside, started the engine, wheeled the car around and drove off. In the dim light, Dickron was unsure of what he had seen, but Topal sure enough sensed it was Dickron before he drove away.

By the time Dickron reached his house he was out of breath. At first, the boys and Mariam all started talking at once until Dickron brought some order to bear. After having heard all the details of their ordeal, he told them how proud he was of the way they had all reacted. Then he went to the cellar and found some stiff cardboard with which to cover the kitchen window opening to keep the chill out. It was already late so they all turned in. The following day Dickron went to the hardware store, bought a sheet of glass cut to size and returning home, installed it.

On Monday morning, the first thing Dickron did was to locate Topal who saw him first and sensed trouble ahead. He forced a smile and nodded his head submissively. Dickron walked over to him and said, "I hear that you gave my wife and children some trouble last night. In fact, you frightened them and you threatened to rape my wife! Is that right?"

"Aw, come on," Topal said, "Do you think I would do such a thing? Maybe I was a little tipsy last night and said something I shouldn't have—I can't remember everything I might have said. Don't forget I got you your job. You owe me and..."

"If I owe you, then I want to pay you back double," Dickron interrupted. Before Topal could see it coming, Dickron grabbed Topal by the throat with both hands in a choke hold, hooked his leg behind Topal's, pushed, and threw him into a fall. It was an old trick he'd learned as a boy. Topal hit the deck and "traveled to the other shore unconscious" as they said in the old country.

That Friday, after work when Dickron went to collect his paycheck, he noticed a folded slip of paper in the envelope, which he couldn't read. When he got home he asked Garo what was written on the slip. Garo read the message to himself. He looked right into his father's eyes and couldn't say a word. His father looked into his son's eyes and knew something was seriously wrong.

"Well, what does it say?" Dickron asked his son.

"It says you're fired from your job," blurted Garo.

Dickron turned pale and his wife asked incredulously, "Fired? Why are you fired, my dear man? What has happened?"

"I really don't know, but I suspect ..." Dickron began.

"Poppa." interrupted Garo, "it says here that your '...employment has been terminated because you have written a letter in which you defame the integrity and reputation of Mr. O'Malley, a manager at Brown and Sharpe.'"

The following day, Mariam bided her time until Dickron had left the house, then she set out on an errand of her own. It was a fairly long and difficult walk for Mariam but she made it to her friend Anahid's house, pushing the baby carriage all the way. Anahid had been a schoolteacher and her English was perfect. She was delightfully surprised when she saw her longtime friend and welcomed her.

Mariam told her the story of her husband's dismissal from his job. The more she revealed, the stronger grew her own suspicions about Topal's and his daughter Julia's involvement in her husband's loss of employment.

Anahid and Mariam got caught up in a detailed discussion until Anahid suggested that both women should personally visit Mrs. O'Malley, wife of the superintendent, and ask for her intervention. Mariam agreed to her suggestion.

Anahid telephoned Mrs. O'Malley after finding her husband's name and title in the directory. Approached by Anahid with a request for an interview, Mrs. O'Malley was gracious in her invitation for the coming Saturday. When she hesitantly asked what this was all about, Anahid said, "Oh, it's a serious matter involving the future of an infant. Only you would understand and be able to help us," and instantly won Mrs. O'Malley's support.

Saturday afternoon, Anahid drove her car, with her passengers, following the directions given to her. Mrs. O'Malley was a dignified woman. She served tea and cookies and soon the topic which had brought them together was broached.

Sitting in Mrs. O'Malley's fine parlor, Mariam explained how her husband Dickron was fired from his job with no questions asked because, supposedly, he had written a note denouncing his boss and calling him dirty names. However, he couldn't have written the note, she explained, because he could neither read nor write English. Therefore, Mariam guessed that Mr. Topalian, seemed to be a likely suspect. But she readily admitted that this was a guess based on recent events and that she didn't have anything resembling the barest kind of evidence.

Yes, Mrs. O'Malley acknowledged, her husband had told her briefly about Dickron and why he was discharged as a result of the letter. "But if, as you say, your husband couldn't write the note, what motive does Mr. Topalian have to write such a note which would result in your husband losing his job?"

Anahid translated her question for Mariam, who indicated that Anahid should respond for her. "Mr. Topalian was instrumental in the decision to hire Dickron, and so he felt that Dickron and his wife owed him a favor in return. However, the favor he asked was unthinkable—he asked for their baby daughter!" Mrs. O'Malley gasped with dismay. Anahid nodded and continued, "Of course, Dickron and his wife refused and it was after this that Mr. Topalian's attitude toward them became threatening. Consequently, they suspected his hand in Dickron's firing," concluded Anahid.

"Ah, I begin to understand what happened," Mrs. O'Malley nodded. "Please excuse me one moment," she said, with a smile of encouragement, and went down the hallway into Mr. O'Malley's study. A few moments later both husband and wife came out and Mrs. O'Malley introduced her husband to the ladies.

Mariam stood up, holding her baby, and Mr. O'Malley was embarrassed for her since obviously she did not know American etiquette. Anahid reached up, tugged at Mariam's sleeve and whispered that she should remain seated in the presence of a gentleman who was showing her such respect for her womanhood. Mariam, whose turn it was for embarrassment, now sat and Mr. O'Malley bowed with a smile to ease her obvious discomfort. She wiped away tears and began to rock her infant to sleep.

Mr. O'Malley said, "This is the letter we are talking about." Handing it to Anahid, he asked her to translate it for Mariam, which she did while the other woman listened intently and when Anahid reached the critical part she stopped for a moment, blushed, and apologized for what she next read: "As for that dumb son–of–a–bitch O'Malley, he doesn't know what in hell he's talking about."

She looked at Mr. O'Malley and said, "Sir, with all due respect, do you really think this letter was written in a man's handwriting? I believe that a woman has written this."

"Well, yes, it could have been—now that you mention it, the penmanship is rather feminine. But what kind of woman would use such language and whom do you know that might write such a letter for Mr. Topalian?" Mr. O'Malley asked.

"That's the mystery," Anahid responded and glancing toward Mariam, continued, "and we've discussed the possibility that Mr. Topalian's daughter, Julia, who speaks and writes perfectly in English, may have written it, at her father's insistence. It seems a logical explanation although we can't prove it."

Mrs. O'Malley and her husband stepped to one side and conferred in lowered voices for a moment, Then Mr. O'Malley turned toward the ladies, saying, "I give you my word that I will give this matter serious consideration."

His wife took Mariam's hand as she reassured her, "Don't worry, my husband is a fair man." When Anahid translated this with a smile and nodded for assent, Mariam felt the weight of the world had fallen from her shoulders.

Mrs. O'Malley asked Mariam for permission to hold and cuddle the baby which made Mariam feel proud. There was a little more talk and many thanks expressed. Mrs. O'Malley gave the baby a final caress and in a very subdued voice whispered to Mariam that everything would be all right and not to worry. "My children are grown and how I miss their babyhood," she said with the faraway look that all loving and good mothers understand. The women left with Mrs. O'Malley cooing "Goodbye" over the baby.

It took a few days to get things together, but Mr. O'Malley remained true to his word. He had Dickron's boss report to him, who also knew Topal well enough to give an objective accounting of both men. Then Topal's boss was summoned, who gave his version of Topal's conduct and it wasn't complimentary. Finally, Topal himself was commanded to appear and present his own view. Mr. O'Malley carefully brought the subject of Topal's daughter into the conversation. At the very beginning of it, Topal grew pale and regained composure with some difficulty. O'Malley skillfully avoided any direct references to Topal's part in all of this, knowing that it would warrant further inquiry in due time.

By the end of the week the postman delivered a specially stamped envelope addressed to Dickron who handed it to Garo and asked for an interpretation. Garo read the message: "Report to your work station next Monday."

His mother, standing nearby, was grateful for whatever Mr. O'Malley had done, because he had done it well. "I am going to church to light a candle for Mr. O'Malley so God will take special care of him. As for that scoundrel, Topal, that's up to God's mercy," she said and made the sign of the cross even for "that scoundrel."

Chapter 12
No Tigers in Africa

Harry had his brother and parents laughing so hard as he recounted what he had said and done that they begged him to say no more. Their aching sides hurt too much from uncontrollable laughter even though the event Harry related had happened some five or six years before when he first started school. The story of his experience only now emerged these many years after the fact. Harry's anecdote always sent anyone who heard it into gales of laughter.

Harry had suffered the same embarrassment and shame that many of those children of the first generation had suffered at the start of their schooling because they had not yet learned some very necessary commonplace words in English. For instance, they did not know what the word *urinate* meant or how to say it and even if they knew they would have been reluctant to utter the word. Such words were considered impolite, dirty, and even profane, so an entire list of euphemisms existed in Armenian to get around the problem but there were no English substitutes that Harry or his classmates had yet learned. As a solution, they created an entire list of their own words in English, for expressing what otherwise would be considered impermissible to mention. When words failed them, the inexperienced children found that appropriate gestures were also a means of successfully expressing themselves.

Harry didn't know how to ask the teacher permission to go to the boys' room so he would sit at his desk suffering for a very long time until the teacher excused the class for a scheduled lavatory break. A few times, when he couldn't hold it back any longer and finally lost control, he was forced to sit in the puddle he had created. He took the problem to Garo who had the good sense to be discreet about it.

He told his kid brother the following secret: "Walk up to the teacher's desk and raise your hand for permission to speak to her. Don't worry, she will give it. As soon as she does, cup your hand in front of your fly and jiggle up and down on your toes. As soon as she says you may leave the room, thank her and march out to the john. Don't run until you're out of sight. Don't repeat these details to anyone else. Keep the secret safe."

The first time Harry put into action Garo's advice, there was no one else in the corridor when Harry ran with maximum speed toward the john, arriving at his destination before he lost control of the high-pressure valves in his system. Having followed his brother's instructions, Harry was surprised at how easy it was and told Garo about it. "Yeah," Garo said, "it always is when you know how. Just don't forget to unbutton your fly."

So during the remainder of his first year in school, Harry never forgot how to jiggle up and down, using his newly learned gymnastics to good advantage. It was one of the more important things he learned pursuing "higher education," and he never quite got over his sense of embarrassment at the memory of it even years later.

Meanwhile, Harry learned to take full advantage of having an older brother with experience, and he soon realized that he could benefit with a little tuning in between Momma and his brother, as they discussed Garo's schoolwork. When he had reached the second grade himself it helped him to sound more learned than he really was.

Harry's brother Garo had suffered during his first year in school. He struggled to communicate with his classmates and teachers and complete his schoolwork in a language foreign to him. As a first-grader, he was given the assignment one day to match pictures with the words which identified them. Of course, Garo spoke Armenian fluently since it was the language spoken at home, and he had also memorized many words in Turkish, some in Kurdish and even in French, just hearing his mother use them, she never realizing that he was all ears. So, Garo could identify the picture of the cat by its Turkish name as well as by its Armenian, but hadn't a clue as to what it might be called in English.

Garo was a bright child and within a short while he not only had learned to speak English but had become an avid reader. However, he did not achieve this without it costing him much grief.

Some of his teachers were frequently surprised when he was called upon to read a passage from a textbook. They and his classmates were often stunned to hear the ease and accuracy with which he pronounced words that were purposefully difficult and polysyllabic in order to test a pupil's progress in reading skills.

Because Garo received the highest marks in reading tests he suffered scornful and jealous looks from many of his classmates. As the kids grew older, teachers wondered about the inequality of results when some pupils, no matter how diligently they studied, were unable to achieve better than average grades. Some even failed outright. Then there were others, like Garo, who despite their disadvantages, became star pupils. This was the other face of democracy in action when teachers had a tough time trying to explain why some failed whereas others passed, although all were supposed to be equal.

Garo was aware of the suspicious looks of his teachers the first few times they heard him read difficult and advanced passages. However, they soon realized that his understanding of the written word was genuine, that Garo had a natural aptitude for vocabulary. Furthermore, his interest in reading was fueled by his favorite books on exploration, foreign travel, and high adventure. Once Garo became aware of the larger world beyond Douglas Avenue, he resolved that someday he would visit the exotic places he was reading about. The dreams and imagination of a young boy foreshadowed the adventures of the man he would become. Things foreign and adventurous now held a powerful attraction for him.

Often, Garo was so bored with the routine class reading assignments that he would place his preferred reading on top of his open textbook. This subterfuge didn't fool one of the teachers, who carefully kept an eye on him and was certain of what he was doing. She noticed that he would quickly finish his assignment, then place his extracurricular reading inside the opened textbook, serving as a cover–up. This went on for some time until the teacher called him to her desk after class one day. She asked, point–blank, "How do you like *The Last of the Mohicans?*" So she knew of his shenanigans, after all! "I won't object as long as you make sure you have finished your assignments and don't say a word to anyone so that the entire class doesn't ask me for the same favor. You are way ahead of the others and in your boredom, you will only find a way to get yourself into some kind of trouble. Do you understand?"

Garo smiled and said, "Yes, I promise. And thanks a million for your kindness." It was the first time he understood that look of kindness in her eyes and he was filled with a gratitude that was hard to explain.

Garo also spent much of his free time reading during after school hours and on weekends. In the intensely cold winter months he spent countless hours at the local library, its delightfully warm reading room a welcome relief from the chilly kitchen at home, where the fire in the coal–burning stove often burned itself out. In fact, on a bitterly cold night, before mother sent the children to bed, she would place a few oven-heated bricks between them and the bed covers.

As his education progressed, Garo became an embarrassment to a few of his teachers because of a bad habit he had developed. If he didn't like a teacher because she seemed too bossy he waited until she mispronounced or misused a word, at which time he repeated the word, pronouncing it correctly in a loud voice or he offered an unappreciated correction of word use: Hence, Sargossa (Sea) should be pronounced *Sargasso*; leopard spots, technically, should only be referred to as leopard's *rosettes*; and when a teacher said, "The lions and tigers in Africa sometimes kill people and eat them," he raised his hand and contradicted her flatly, insisting there are no tigers in Africa.

Responding with a demeaning manner, the teacher challenged him to prove it by class the next day. Several of the kids broke out in laughter, which shamed Garo and provoked the teacher to an anger the pupils had not yet seen. As soon as school let out Garo hurried to the public library.

His favorite librarian was on duty and she asked him what the matter was and he told her about the challenge. The librarian said, "I don't know about this so let's have a look, shall we?" and walked with him to the reference section and quickly found the right volume. She read aloud, "Contrary to popular opinion, tigers are not found in the continent of Africa but only in Asia," and continued for a few paragraphs more.

"There, that should be enough to make your point," she said, "but you had better copy this text and write down the page number and name of the author. Good luck, and let me know how you make out."

"Thank you a million times," Garo gratefully responded.

On the following morning before the school doors had opened he sneaked through an unlocked side door and hurried to his classroom where he conspicuously placed a small bag of jelly beans on his teacher's desk. A short while later after the teacher had called her noisy classroom to order, she noticed the candy, with its attached note, on her desk. Having first silently read the note to herself, she proceeded to read the brief note aloud to the class. The teacher was embarrassed, to say the least, but she thanked Garo, saying, "All these years I never knew that there were no tigers in Africa. I think we owe Garo a vote of thanks," and she applauded, encouraging the class to join in. Now it was Garo who was embarrassed when many of the kids joined in the applause.

In a few days most of the short–lived hot admiration for Garo by his schoolmates cooled down to lukewarm. At least, however, Garo was not surprised, having experienced this on– again–off–again experience before.

The Armenians knew this as the go–and–die phenomenon or in their own words: "Go and die and when you come back then I can love you again." Most of the kids had learned this euphemistic expression early in their young lives because Armenian mothers used the phrase so often.

They knew by this time that coming back after dying was impossible so they laughed when a teacher used a phrase in English, "You only live once," not realizing how it would be construed by her students. They wondered how the teacher had become bilingual and when the kids laughed she grew angry, thinking that the kids were laughing at her, and so demanded that they stay after school. The kids wondered what they had done wrong to receive such punishment. Eventually, the news leaked out and after some mothers who knew English complained to the principal, a faculty meeting was held and the said faculty was enlightened. Nobody knew who had done the tattling but the class had a pretty good suspicion.

Chapter 13

The Untutored Peasant

Dandy Andy, as he was called, was a happy–go–lucky kid and was a prankster at heart. One afternoon during recess in the schoolyard he saw the edge of Garo's handkerchief sticking out of his pocket. He gingerly lifted it out as the boys' line marched back to the classroom. A few moments later as Andy passed by Garo's desk, he tossed the hankie onto Garo's lap. Andy giggled at the look of surprise on Garo's face, who hadn't the slightest notion of what had happened earlier. Garo made his plan to get even with his classmate on the following day.

The boys were in the schoolyard again. Garo deliberately tripped himself against Andy's body, and stepped on his foot as he yanked out the small jackknife suspended from Andy's belt. Under the pressure of bodily impact, Andy couldn't feel Garo lifting the knife. Later, when Andy felt for his knife it was gone. In a surge of panic he nervously grabbed at his waistline and still could not find it. Garo, in a fit of laughter, asked, "Is this what you're looking for?" and he returned the knife to Andy. It was Garo's turn to gloat but his glee was short–lived.

From a classroom window overlooking the playground, Mr. Flynn, the principal, had been watching the boys standing in line. Now he began wrapping sharply on the glass. Hearing the sharp clicking sound, Garo turned around to find that Mr. Flynn was pointing his finger straight at him, beckoning him forward. Garo sensed something seriously wrong. He had always felt that Mr. Flynn did not like him and often picked on him for frivolous reasons. What now? he wondered.

Garo was frightened. This was the third time he had been called in for a "conference" in as many months. He was sure, by now, that Mr. Flynn was picking on him for no good reason.

Garo had not mentioned a word of this to his parents.

Mr. Flynn, with his famous angry scowl, beat around the bush for a few moments and then asked Garo why he had pick–pocketed Andy. Oh, is that all, Garo thought to himself. That could be explained. He relaxed a bit and said, "Yesterday, Andy picked my pocket and today I was getting even with him. I wasn't stealing his knife. I returned it to him. You can ask him."

It was the sort of trick all the kids played on each other, but Mr. Flynn clearly did not buy that answer. This kid was not only a thief, he was a liar also, he thought. "Garo, I want to see you and your father for a conference in my office tomorrow after school."

Armenian kids got more than a fair share of *odar* prejudice and discrimination, Garo thought. Was this more of the same? It was always a question for which there was no simple answer and Garo had been warned by his parents never to judge odars hastily because, like Armenians, there were more good than bad among them. A clear–cut answer was never easy. Human nature was human nature and the trick was to learn how to live with it, Garo had been taught by his parents.

The following afternoon at the close of another grueling workday, Dickron walked from the factory to his son's school. Waiting with Garo for Mr. Flynn to return to his office, Dickron studied a framed picture on the principal's desk. The photo was obviously of Mr. Flynn, his wife, two daughters, and a son. So he, too, was human after all, Dickron mused.

Garo glanced at his father who was grimy with dirt, unshaven and obviously tired from his heavy labors of the day. He was staring at the photo and for a moment how Garo wished his father's appearance could rival that of his principal's.

The door opened and Mr. Flynn walked in. Dickron instantly yanked his work hat off his head and reflexively bowed his head as if he were back in the old country. Unconsciously, he had paid a sign of obeisance to a man he perceived as being more important than himself. That's how his early years as a boy had conditioned him. When he looked up he saw perplexity and embarrassment on Mr. Flynn's face at the deference he was shown. Was Mr. Flynn not as tough as he appeared?

Mr. Flynn's sense of embarrassment was quickly followed by a fleeting moment of compassion for this poor man who confronted him. Mr. Stepanian was a reminder of how his own father probably felt when he came to this country. Compassion, Mr. Flynn briefly considered, was the real ground for the brotherhood of man.

Dickron was also embarrassed. For a moment he had felt he was back in the old country intimidated by fear, persecution, and terror, by the appearance of a well-dressed man who was not a phantom Turk but a civilized American. He was the principal of the school providing his son with an education. Dickron was ashamed to present himself as a foreigner, unable to understand what was being said between his son and his principal. He felt a choking in his throat from the iron dust which had irritated him nearly all day long. He wished for a glass of water to quench his thirst and shame. He wondered why his son had to be here to witness this humiliation.

How different Mr. Flynn appeared in his white shirt, fancy necktie and finely tailored suit. He was a perfect symbol of sophistication and modernity. He belonged in this world and in comparing himself to Mr. Flynn, Dickron could not free himself from his own self-abnegation.

Mr. Flynn said, in a stern voice, "Young man, tell your father what you did in the schoolyard and why you did it." When Garo tried to explain what he had done, his father, like most parents, believed his son could not be guilty of such a charge. A thief? Impossible! Insulting!

Dickron kept his head bowed this time to hide his rage. He knew that this gentleman thought of him as an untutored peasant, but that didn't bother him too much because there was some truth to that. But did that gentleman think for a moment that this peasant had not raised an honest son? This is what offended him.

Mr. Stepanian said something to his son and Mr. Flynn asked the boy, "What did your father say?"

Garo squirmed rather than answer. His father said sternly, "Tell him what I said." and looked right into Mr. Flynn's eyes as his son carried out the order.

"My father said he's sure that you would never raise your son to lie. Why do you think he would not do the same for *his* son?"

Mr. Flynn winced and didn't know quite what to say. So he said nothing. He stood up indicating that the conference was over. Garo took his father's extended hand. Father and son walked out quietly.

Chapter 14
The Green Snake

Garo and Harry walked nearly all around the far end of Leonard's Pond before they agreed on where they could find the best place of entry at the water's edge. They cautiously took a stride or two into the water and immediately saw what they were looking for—a large white glob of a translucent mass suspended in the water. It was a mass of tadpoles not yet metamorphosed into baby frogs.

"Aw, shucks," Harry muttered, "we're too early. How long do you think it'll take?"

"Maybe another five days or so. Let's go to the cemetery and see if we can find something better," Garo said. So the boys worked their way back to the top of the hill, made a sharp turn and headed for the cemetery.

Garo, having taken this walk before, easily found the right path through a labyrinth of tombstones in endless numbers. The carved dates indicated they had been there long before the First World War. Soon, the boys reached a place where the untrimmed grass was tall and swaying gently in the breeze. "What now?" Harry asked.

"Just follow me and watch what I do," Garo said as he reached down to grab a large flat boulder and turned it over. "Ah, ha!" he exclaimed. "This is what we're after and it's a beauty, indeed." It was a garter snake, with a bright green sheen, nearly fifteen inches long and a little thicker than an Italian Parodi cigar. It began to uncoil slowly now that Garo had removed the stone slab covering it. Bathed in full sunshine, the reptile began its sinuous crawl forward. Quicker than it started to move, Garo's hand shot out and he grabbed it behind its head. He reached into his side pocket, removed the denim sack in it, shook it open, dropped the squirming creature into it and tied a knot in the top of the sack with a piece of string. "Okay," he said to his brother, "it's your turn now." Before long they captured another snake and walking briskly, made for home.

By the time they both went to sleep that night, Garo had it all figured out. He knew exactly what he wanted to do with his snake.

During that school year he had been assigned a seat next to Margie Nelson, who was truly a lovely girl. Moreover, she was highly intelligent. Most of all, she was innocently flirtatious with him. Suddenly, he realized how much he really liked her in return. Was this, in fact, why he had avoided speaking to her in order to convince himself that he had no interest in girls at all? On occasion he had heard other boys called sissies for being too friendly with girls. Moreover, he knew that older people often talked about girls who seemed bawdy and had bad reputations. Boys were warned to stay away from them.

Garo was confused by such talk. How could girls be called bawdy and sinful on the one hand and yet parents insisted that they be respected and adored at the same time? In either case there was a lot to be learned about girls but when he asked his mother or father for an explanation, they would invariably reply, "You will learn later when you grow up." Later seemed so far away.

Garo wanted to capture Margie's attention, yet do it so that she wouldn't suspect that he was in love with her. He suddenly realized the true value of his little green snake and began to thoughtfully formulate a plan.

Just after recess, Garo found his opportunity. He recalled that when she came indoors from recess Margie usually opened her lunch box to take out her comb for a quick brush of her windblown hair. Garo darted to the cloakroom, found Margie's lunch box among the others on the cloakroom shelf, opened the lid and quickly transferred the snake into her lunch box.

Garo rushed back to his desk, sat down and without blinking, he opened his book and pretended to read. From the corner of his eye, he observed Margie enter the room and go to the cloakroom for her lunch box. She took it to her desk, where she opened the lid—Margie let out the most terrifying screams, which rose above the hubbub of children returning from recess, the sound of her terror reverberating throughout the building. Margie slid out of her chair onto the floor in a dead faint. Instantly, the classroom was thrown into pandemonium and doors further down the hallway were thrown wide as children, teachers, and janitors came flying out to escape what sounded like the end of the world.

It never occurred to Garo what his innocent prank might lead to. What it led to minutes later were sirens blaring out their eerie warning of the earth's sudden demise, from the direction of the fire station, only a block away from the school. Soon, news about a disaster blanketed the neighborhood with fantastic rumors circulating about what everyone imagined had happened.

Garo took his usual seat the following day at school and thought that Margie's apparent aloofness was a sign of her anger toward him. "She probably hates me," Garo thought miserably, "as the cause of her fainting spell." He thought she seemed sullen because she hadn't given him her usual sunny smile. He felt ashamed for having overdone his prank.

The funny thing about it was that Margie was in love with Garo and although he had scared her witless, she was prepared to forgive him. "But why is he avoiding me, this morning?" she wondered. For different reasons of their own, each thought the other was offended. For a couple of days, Margie and Garo would sneak a furtive glance at one another to see if there was a hint of forgiveness, any indication of a change of heart, or the suggestion of a warm friendly smile, hoping for any sign that things had returned to just the way they used to be.

It was Margie who confessed first to having misread Garo's mind. Then Garo apologized for having misread Margie's mind. Then they laughed at the comedy of their errors and at the end of the day found themselves walking home together, hand in hand. "Girls aren't so peculiar, after all. They're okay in their own way," Garo mused. Ah, the wonder of first love!

Chapter 15
Honor Thy Family

The Armenian word, *Barron* was pronounced to rhyme with "Bah–rawn" with the *r* rolled hard in Armenian. It was a title of respect used by anyone addressing a man with graying hair, older than oneself.

Barron Boghos was from a province of Armenia where the vernacular was so different from elsewhere in the same culture that an urban Armenian would not understand his rustic compatriot easily, and vice versa. The Armenian Mr. Paul, or Barron Boghos, was an elderly man, short of stature, heavy in the paunch, and bald–headed. He was reputed to be one of the stingiest men on Douglas Avenue. None of the kids liked him because he frequently picked on them for the least excuse.

Sunday afternoon during family dinner after church, Harry and Garo were in a discussion about Mr. Boghos or Mr. Paul. In a careless moment Harry referred to him as a "stingy, thieving, and lying donkey." Dickron heard that remark and immediately took him to task.

"Never let me hear you talk that way about Mr. Boghos again. Do you hear me? He is an old man and you have been taught to respect your elders." From the tone of his father's voice, Harry knew that Poppa was furious.

"Poppa," Harry started to say, "You always tell us to hold high the family honor. That's all I tried to do when I saw what Baron Boghos was up to..."

"What was he doing?" his father interrupted with anger.

Harry instantly realized he had said too much. He gritted his teeth and squirmed.

"I asked you a question. What did Barron Boghos do or say?" Dickron repeated, as he angrily watched his son squirm, a sure sign that he would stubbornly say no more and prefer to face the consequences.

"My son, the point is that he is years older than both of us. He is to be respected because of his age. He is entitled to that because that is the law of our God and our people and you know that. No matter how wrong you think he is, he's still worthy of our respect. It is a matter of family honor. Do you understand?"

Dickron felt his wife squeezing his arm. It was a signal, a means of silently pleading that her son be spared a spanking. When he saw the look of mercy in his wife's eyes, Dickron relented and told his son to go to his bedroom and stay there. Harry knew his mother had rescued him again and as he walked out, he gave her a sideways glance of gratitude.

The next day Harry played William Tell with his bow and arrows. His class had recently read the story of Tell, whose bravery and marksmanship had impressed him.

Carpet stores displayed their large carpets rolled around bamboo poles and kids were always on the lookout for them. Harry had acquired several of the shorter poles. When split lengthwise the poles had quite a spring to them. Harry had already split one and needed only the bowstring's attachment. This kind of "archery" was a common form of play among the kids.

Harry placed a short folding ladder against the fence separating his family's backyard from that of Barron Boghos's, and draped a large section of cardboard box over the ladder, creating a backdrop. He stepped back about fifteen feet and loosed an arrow which thwacked right through the flimsy barrier into the fence board behind it.

He called Garo to witness his next deed. This time, he picked up and balanced on the ladder three overripe pears which had fallen from the tree. The only trouble was that they had fallen over the fence from Barron Boghos's tree into Momma's garden. However, Harry reasoned that the moment those pears hit terrra firma they belonged to his family and not to Barron Boghos. So showing off his prowess for his older brother, Harry took careful aim and the target exploded as his arrow found its mark. The remaining pears were likewise dispatched.

The following morning, Harry went out early and collected several of the overripe pears to place on the ladder and played William Tell some more. He had a jolly good time of it but he didn't know that Barron Boghos was spying on him from behind his kitchen windows.

Harry went out for marksmanship again in the late afternoon and to his surprise he saw that the pears he had left behind were all gone. There was only one possible answer: Barron Boghos.

Harry kept a sharp lookout early on Saturday morning and his suspicion was confirmed when he espied Barron Boghos. The Barron was armed with a homemade lance, a broom handle with a sharpened nail projecting from one end. He was leaning over the fence and stabbing the nail into the scattered pears on the ground, spearing fruit which had fallen on the Stepanians' property. As he retrieved the pears, he slipped them off his lance into a pail. Since he knew nothing about archery, what else could Barron Boghos possibly do with rotten pears? Harry wondered. At least, Harry put them to good use as he imagined William Tell might have done.

Harry heard his mother setting the breakfast table, went to her and pleaded that she step into his bedroom, even though Garo was barely awake. She could easily see from behind the curtain. There was the Barron hard at work plucking stabbed pears off his lance. He was even now covering wider territory.

"Dear God," uttered Mariam. "I cannot believe what my eyes are seeing."

"Momma," Harry said, "please stay here and don't let Barron Boghos see you."

"Why? Where are you going?" she asked but Harry was already gone, on his way out to the backyard.

No sooner did Barron Boghos take his pears indoors than Harry made a decision instantly as kids are wont to do. It was only about fifteen paces to the fence, which he reached in a flash like lightning. He crouched low behind it and not a moment too soon. Barron Boghos had returned and his lance tip soon appeared over the fence. As he pushed the length of it over the top of the fence, Harry suddenly sprang up and grabbed the lance. In the same instant, he gave his version of Tarzan's victory cry of the bull ape.

For a second, the startled Barron Boghos lost his grip on the lance, which Harry easily tore from his hand. Harry brandished it overhead and fled like a deer. His mother had witnessed all that transpired.

"I couldn't tell Poppa about Barron Boghos the thief, until I had proof and here it is," he said tossing the lance on the floor. "I don't think that what Barron Boghos has been doing is anything that can be called honorable. I'm just trying to defend our family honor. Those pears are on our ground. If I can't defend our honor against this crook then when can I defend it?" He smiled with a look of satisfaction. How well he had presented his case!

"Don't worry," his mother promised, "I will take care of this. Join your brother in the kitchen."

She went back to her bedroom where Dickron was already up. His sleep had been disturbed and he wanted to know what was going on. Mariam asked him to step into the children's bedroom, where she cautiously drew the curtains back a bit, telling her husband, "I guess this is what Harry wanted to talk to you about. He said he was defending the family honor and that Barron Boghos is a thief after all."

After several moments of silence as all this began to make sense, Dickron said, "Well, they are his pears, after all." But it sounded like he was trying to convince himself rather than his wife.

"But they landed on our ground," she argued.

"I guess only a lawyer can straighten this out," he said, "and I am not about to see one. For now, let's eat breakfast."

Harry and Garo were already seated when their parents joined them. Dickron said grace, then in silence everyone proceeded to eat what Mariam set before them. When they had finished breakfast, the family waited for Dickron to speak. After what seemed like a long time of waiting respectfully for him to commence speaking, he said, "Your mother has told me what you reported to her. She says that she saw Barron Boghos retrieving the fallen pears. He believes they belong to him because they grew on his tree. You believe they are yours, or ours, because they landed in our garden, but in any event, you didn't say anything to me." Addressing Harry, he asked, "That is correct, isn't it, my son?"

"Yes," said Harry, "I did it for the family's honor. That man was robbing us of what belonged to us, not to him."

There was silence for several minutes until Dickron spoke again. "I am not so interested in what you claim to be true, or what Barron Boghos has said or done. I am concerned about what you haven't considered—and never mind him." Mariam and her sons looked at each other somewhat puzzled. What was Poppa driving at?

"You are my son," Dickron said. "I am proud of you. You defended the family honor. You had courage to do it your way." He admonished his son gently, saying, "I am not scolding you for that. Barron Boghos may be as bad as you say. Nevertheless, why didn't you go to him and say you were sorry for offending him? Never mind what he did. It would have been a gift of your kindness to him. Kindness is never wrong. If he refused to listen, the dishonor was a sin around his neck, not yours, as they say in the old country. Do you know what I am trying to tell you? Do you understand?"

"I think so," Harry said, and he rose from the table and rushed into his father's arms. It occurred to Dickron that he hadn't experienced such an affectionate outburst from his younger son in a long time. He swooped him up and hugged him back. "I will try to say I'm sorry to Barron Boghos tomorrow after school," Harry resolved, hoping he would not lose his courage by then.

Something didn't feel right to him when he went out after school on the following day to see Barron Boghos. He stopped for a few minutes to look around and suddenly his eye caught sight of it—the pear tree. He was looking right at it, only it didn't look right. Suddenly it dawned on him. The branch laden with pears that had hung out over the fence, was gone! Where it had once been attached to the trunk, there was now a sawed-off stump. He walked close to the fence and looked over the top. There was the branch lying on the ground on Barron Boghos's side of the fence with sawdust spread around it.

Harry hurried home and called his mother to the window. "You see what Barron Boghos has done?" he indignantly asked his mother, and jerked his thumb in the direction of the tree, newly missing one of its limbs.

"Oh, no, not more trouble," Mariam groaned as she saw the remaining blunt stub of the freshly sawed-off branch.

"What do we do now?" Harry asked angrily. "What he's done to that poor tree is worse than anything I've done to a few rotten pears."

"Only your father can answer that. Let's wait until he comes home," Momma decided.

After Dickron came home and they were eating dinner, he

observed, "I see that Barron Boghos has cut a branch from the pear tree."

"Oh, you saw it?" Mariam asked.

"How could I fail to see it?" he replied.

"Do I still have to tell him that I'm sorry?" Harry asked. "Look at what he's done to that poor tree."

"What do you think you should do?" his father countered.

"I think I should forget it. He's a bad man for cutting a branch off his own tree just to get even. Like you say, Poppa, 'Let the sin be on his neck.' We're not guilty. He is!"

Dickron smiled and then he said, "I have a better idea for you. I want you to be a gentleman, not a *virenee* (wilderness man). I want you to teach him a good lesson in forgiveness, not revenge." He reached into his pocket and removing a quarter, said, "Take this and go with your brother to the store. Buy a pint of ice cream for us. It costs ten cents. With the remaining fifteen cents buy some pears. You should be able to get two or three of them of the best variety. On the way home, stop at Barron Boghos's, knock on his door and when he opens it give him the bag. Smile and say, 'We are sorry this is the best we can do for now; thank you for not refusing us.' Say nothing else and before he can respond, immediately walk away."

"What if he doesn't take it?" Harry asked.

"Put them on the step," his father replied, "and walk away. Let the sin…"

"…be on his neck," Harry and Garo chimed in.

When the boys left to run their errand, Dickron hugged his wife and said, "Woman, I am so proud of you for the sons you have given me."

"My man," Mariam said, "I am so proud of you as their father, for setting an example of charitable conduct."

"That's a fine compliment," he answered with a grin, but he pondered what lessons of life he might share next with his sons as they met life head–on with boisterous enthusiasm, experiencing the inevitable growing pains along the way. With fatherly guidance, they would indeed grow up to become honorable men.

Before long, Harry was struggling once again with the issue of charitable behavior, which his parents prized so highly. His angry feelings toward Barron Boghos lingered. Forgiveness was more difficult than he had imagined. Harry felt disgruntled and he soon found an opportunity to vent his frustrations.

His teacher, Miss O'Neil, gave an assignment to the class in penmanship and spelling, asking her pupils to write a brief essay on any topic. She reminded them that proper nouns, including names of people or places, should be capitalized. Harry jumped to the task, beginning an essay about Barron Boghos, who had been on his mind for several days since Harry had seen him spearing fallen pears from the Stepanian's garden. Harry left nothing to the imagination, referring to Barron Boghos as "stingy, a thief, and nasty."

That evening at home, Miss O'Neil graded the essays which she had collected from her pupils. She read Harry's story about Barron Boghos with interest, fascinated as always with any insights into the cultural heritage of others besides that of her own Irish people. Miss O'Neil knew that most Armenian families were devoutly religious and proud of their heritage, especially of the fact that Armenia had officially become the first Christian nation in history in 301 AD. Why St. Patrick, the Irish priest of her faith, she mused, wasn't born until eighty-six years later! So, Miss O'Neil wasn't surprised that Boghos was a popular name among Armenians, parents often naming their sons after Saint Paul. Throughout several years of teaching, she had known at least a dozen Pauls, or Boghoses among her Armenian pupils. Unfortunately, Miss O'Neil ruefully acknowledged, almost all the teachers pronounced Boghos as Bogus because they couldn't pronounce the gh sound.

In Harry's essay, he did not refer to his neighbor as Mr. Boghos, but rather as Barron Boghos. Miss O'Neil thought about the barons of European culture and reflected that the pronunciation of barron might be the same as that for baron. Could it be that both titles meant the same thing, and if so, could Harry's villainous Barron be an aristocrat?

The next day, Miss O'Neil called Harry aside as the other students left the room for the playground. "Harry, how do you translate the meaning of the word Barron?"

"Barron means sir or mister," Harry answered. "Is that all? Can I go out now?"

"Of course. Thank you, Harry." So, Miss O'Neil smiled to herself, Mr, Paul was only an ordinary villain after all.

Chapter 16
Aerial Combat

Garo went to the barber shop to get his hair cut, saying "Hello" as he entered, to Mr. Azarig the barber. He took a seat and flipped through some magazines while waiting for the person before him to get trimmed. His eyes caught sight of a World War I magazine picture of a German war ace in flight. Next to it was another picture of a German war ace leaning out of the cockpit with an aerial bomb in his hand, taking aim at a target far below.

The story began with a description of the aces—one was Baron Manfred von Richtoffen the other was Max Immelman. Garo was nearly glued to his chair reading the breathtaking accounts of these flying warriors and their exploits. He was halfway through the story when it was his turn and the barber called him. When the barber finished, Garo returned to the article but Mr. Azarig was kind enough to tell him he could take the magazine home.

Garo left the barber shop and walked down Douglas Avenue. As he drew near the bakery, he caught sight of two figures scurrying around the side of the building.

One of the boys looked furtively over his shoulder and seeing Garo, placed his forefinger to his lips and then waved at Garo, beckoning him to join them. Garo recognized his friend and trotted over to meet the boys. He guessed what was happening. In fact, he had participated in the ritual himself at an earlier time. As Garo turned the corner of the building, sure enough, there were a number of boys gathered next to the brick chimney of the bakery. In the lineup of boys, he saw that Hovhaness Chebookian, known as "Johnny–Cue–Stick," was at the head of the line. He was urinating as high as he could on the hot surface of the bakery's huge brick chimney.

Inside the bakery, bread was browning in the wood-fuelled brick oven. The baker was rolling out pieces of dough to make Armenian bread, a circular cracker-thin bread, nearly two feet in diameter, and sprinkled with sesame seeds. The bread baked quickly, small numerous bubble blisters forming on its surface. The boys had always called them "sewer covers."

The ambient air became malodorous with the scent of hot urine. The baker instantly realized what was taking place. He flung the shop door wide open and gave chase, brandishing a broom and bellowing, "Satan soured your mother's milk the day you were born," and other epithets. But the boys had already escaped over the iron fence behind the bakery. There was nothing the baker could do, so he continued to swear out loud as he walked back to his work.

After the boys regrouped, they began to argue about who had peed the highest. Garo drifted back a little closer to Chikee and in a subdued voice asked, "Can you come by my house anytime soon?" and Chikee's answer was, "Sure." Garo then approached another of the boys, Hago, and spoke quietly with him for a moment, saying, "Pass the word along," before casually walking away.

Three or four days passed. Garo planned to make a speed wagon and was in the backyard sawing two-by-fours in half for the project, when Chikee and Hago, with a couple of their buddies, hove into view. They waved hello to Garo who returned their greeting and asked where they were going. "We're coming to see you," the boys answered and Chikee added, "You wanted to see us, so here we are," and pounded his fist into his baseball glove.

Garo invited his friends to take a seat on the garden bench. Soon, they were involved in small talk until Garo said, "I need ya to help me and I'll make it up to you but first you must swear on your honor that you'll tell no one what you're about to see, no questions asked. Can I trust you?"

Sensing that something important was about to be revealed and feeling proud of Garo's faith in them, his chums gladly agreed. "Yeah," the boys promised. "You know you can. What do ya want us to do?"

Garo curtly said, "Follow me," and led the way into his house. He signaled the fellows to silently follow him on tiptoe up the stairs. His chums wondered what this was all about. They reached the attic and walked into the room and Garo quietly closed the door. He motioned to the boys to sit and reached for one of several empty quart-sized glass milk bottles sitting on the dusty floor. He fumbled with his trouser's fly buttons and barely made it in time to urinate into the bottle and when he had finished, passed the bottle to Chikee. Chikee and the other fellows were flabbergasted but took their turns, expecting an explanation afterward.

By this time his chums suspected that Garo had lost his mind. They had never before seen such bizarre behavior on his part. Having completed their mission in the attic, the boys wordlessly followed Garo downstairs to the closet beside the front door. The closet contained an ice box from which Garo removed bottles of sarsaparilla soda pop. He also grabbed several small bars of sugared peanut bars, frozen solid. Garo led the way outdoors.

Garo passed out the soda and candy to his chums, who could not believe their good fortune. They were lying on the grassy edge of the garden when Chikee asked the question: "Aw, come on Garo. What the heck is this all about?"

"No questions, remember? But I have one for you. Would you be willing to pee in the bottles again, later today?"

"Okay," the boys agreed in unison. They returned later that afternoon and stealthily climbed upstairs to the attic. Relieving their full bladders, the boys succeeded in filling another milk bottle. After some time, the ritual was recommenced, which completed the call to duty. The bottles, now filled, were placed in the center of the sill of the attic's only window, which caught the full power of the sunshine. Garo produced candy bars, paid off his bill to the team, and showed the boys out.

Chikee was impatient. For a second time, he asked Garo, "When are you going to tell us what they're for?"

Garo promised, "I'll tell you as soon as the pee is ripe enough." The following day, Garo was up a little earlier than usual, reading. When Harry showed up to sneak a look at what Garo was reading, Garo showed him the German war aces magazine from the barber shop.

"Do you see what Immelmann is doing?" Garo asked.

"Yeah," Harry said, "He's gonna blast the daylights out of us."

"Well, that's close enough," Garo asserted.

"Close enough for what?" Harry asked.

"You'll see. Today is Saturday, right? So tomorrow will be Sunday and time for church. I'll need your help then. Will you come upstairs to the attic when I wake you?"

"What for?" asked Harry.

"It's a secret. You'll see."

"Yeah, I know. With you, everything is a secret."

"Yes or no, for the last time?" Garo asked.

"You know darn well I won't refuse you," Harry replied.

"You know very well I won't leave you out, either," Garo said. "May the sin be on the neck of whoever chickens out first."

It was about half–past–seven the following morning when Garo awoke and roused Harry. Garo shook his brother wide-awake and whispering "Shush" a half–dozen times along the way, dragged him upstairs to the attic.

Taking two or three deep breaths as he entered the room, Harry gagged and moaned and finally was able to exclaim, "What is that awful stink?"

Garo clapped his hand over his brother's mouth and pointed his finger to where the bottles stood, filled to the top with a golden yellow–tinted liquid. "That's what you're smelling," he whispered, muffling his laughter. "Don't you recognize the smell of pee–pee?"

Garo reached over and grabbed some twenty pound paper sacks he'd collected earlier and left on a rickety chair. He placed two sacks inside each other, sat back with a smile and said, "this is gonna work out just swell."

"Do ya remember how Barron Boghos cut the pear tree branch that hung over our fence? Well, it's time for getting even and the article I read about Immelmann and Richtofen gave me an idea about how we might do that."

"Well, how come you didn't tell me? Harry complained.

"If you remember, I tried several times but you were too busy, you said. So I gave up on you. If you listen now, I'll tell you for the last time, so pay attention. What does Barron Boghos do every Sunday morning, about nine o'clock? He passes beneath our attic window on his way to church, right?

Aerial Combat

Well, the way I see it, this gives us the best opportunity for an ambush. Bro, you're going to be Immelmann, I'll be Richtofen and we're going to bomb Barron Boghos this morning."

"With what?" asked Harry in astonishment.

"With pee! According to my experiments, in the time it takes to say, 'bombs away' this bag of pee will land on him and break open. So get ready. Here he comes now. I'll fill the bag, you open the window."

Harry pushed the window up and the boys positioned themselves on either side, Garo holding the loaded bag. "When you say, 'bombs away,' I let 'er go," instructed Garo.

Barron Boghos was old, heavy set, and leaning on his cane, walked with a noticeable limp. His suit was shiny from too many ironings and his black derby hat had seen its heyday long before. As he passed beneath the window, the boys released their bomb.

They couldn't resist the temptation of watching it on its way down. The timing was perfect. It landed, exploding right on the Barron's derby. It was a spectacular hit.

"Let's get out of here, fast!" Garo said, barely above a whisper.

"What do we do, now?" his brother asked with a pounding heart as they dashed for the door.

"Just run like hell. Head for the park," Garo advised since he didn't know what else to do.

They spent the remainder of the afternoon playing ball at Hopkins Park with a few of their friends. It was late in the afternoon when they returned home. Garo and Harry knew immediately that they were in serious trouble. Their father sat in his chair, holding the Armenian daily newspaper in his hands, but he was reading it up–side–down. "Boys," he said, with a scowl on his face, "let me get to the point. Barron Bohgos' grandson was here to say that this morning you dumped water out the attic window and drenched his grandfather."

Garo jumped in quickly. "Poppa," he said, "it was my fault. I spilled it."

"No," Harry contradicted. "it was my fault."

"Well," their father said, "since both of you were involved, the punishment goes to both of you at five whacks each."

"But Poppa," Harry insisted, "it was my fault and I don't..."

As their father started to remove his belt, Garo furtively

kicked Harry sharply in the shin. Garo had glanced at his father's face and knew this would be more ritual than punishment. Poppa was not as angry as he appeared to be.

When the boys were left alone, Harry asked, "Why did you kick me when I was only trying to help you? You hurt me more than Poppa did, by turning on me."

"I kicked you because you didn't see what was about to happen. When you blabbed that it was your fault, instead of mine, you opened the way for further questioning. The Barron couldn't admit that it was pee which doused him. If you'd confessed the truth, my guess is, you'd have gotten us into deeper water."

Relenting, Harry agreed, "We would've been in water over our heads!"

"Over our heads?" laughed Garo. *"Gusses ou togh goodas?"* (Or in Armenian, You say and let it go at that?)

Chapter 17
Picnic Armenian Style

Huncho was a taciturn old–timer from Sivas province, noted for its Armenian population, culture and history. He had narrowly missed the genocide as a young man although his first wife had not been so fortunate. She had been gang–raped by Turkish soldiers before she was finally bayonetted to death.

He married again and joined his compatriots in Providence, to raise a new family. When the Great Depression closed down the factory where he worked, he tried his hand at selling ice cream, nuts, and candy. His store was a very little place and a very big flop. He would read nearly all day and finally close shop to go home. On a good day he sold maybe a small amount of various nuts used in making old–country pastries. In fact, Huncho guessed he had made a mistake in his choice of business shortly after the first week of it or the lack of it.

One afternoon he decided to go home a little earlier than usual. But before he could close up, he was a little surprised when Little Roogie walked into the store and kept gawking at the candy display. Mr. Huncho did not know, of course, the real reason why Roogie was there. His buddies, including Garo and Harry, had wagered that he could not swindle Mr. Huncho out of a bag of candy. It was a deal that only Satan could have engineered. "Vot voud you like?" Mr. Huncho asked with a phoney grin and Roogie answered with an equally phoney grin, "Candy," and stared at all the goodies under glass.

"Vitch vons?" asked Mr. Huncho.

"These vons," mimicked Roogie, cupping both hands into a circle as large as his finger tips allowed barely touching each other. Mr. Huncho reflexively smiled at the goodly amount

Roogie's hand gestures suggested. He held his breath as soon as Roogie held his tongue.

"Some more?" asked Mr. Huncho.

"Yes, over there," Roogie said moving his hands to the right and moved them again and again.

After the third and fourth handful of candy, Mr. Huncho grew somewhat apprehensive. It suddenly dawned on him to ask this kid if that was not enough. How would he pay for all this? When the kid made no effort to reach for money, Mr. Huncho, suspecting the worst, abruptly gave Roogie the cash register receipt and asked, "How you pay for all this?" Roogie stole a glance at the doorway, which was a serious mistake; Mr. Huncho finally got the full picture. Again, he asked Roogie, "Vere is your money?" with anger in his voice.

This broke the impasse for which Roogie had been waiting. Digging deeply into both empty pockets and pulling them out with empty shakes he said, "But I have no money," and waved the inverted empty pockets again for good measure. He correctly anticipated Mr. Huncho's next move.

Mr. Huncho could no longer stand the humiliation inflicted on him by this brat acting like a holdup bandit. "You sum una beech!" shouted Mr. Huncho as he quickly bent under the counter, grabbed a sawed–off mop handle hidden there, and pulled it out. Before he got his footing he swung down mightily. It threw him off balance. As he tripped, Mr. Huncho's aim went wild and on the downstroke with his emergency cudgel, he smashed the thick glass shelf atop the brass keys of the register.

Roogie was nearly out the door as Mr. Huncho slipped and crashed to the floor. Two steps past the wreckage, Roogie threw open the door of the store and leaped outside. By this time half of the street corner gang had gathered to witness the commotion.

In a moment of inspiration, Harry rushed forward and pushed his peggy swatter through the brass curved handles of the double doors, to great effect. Years before, one of those doors had been permanently fastened shut. The working door was now barred by the broomstick peggy swatter and did not budge despite Mr. Huncho's efforts to escape. He was trapped inside his store.

Mr. Huncho was livid with rage as he rapped on the glass and rattled the door for help from any passerby. The trolley had just passed by on Douglas Avenue and that meant a half–hour wait for the next one. He was a prisoner until some kind soul came to his rescue. But the passersby either did not understand what the window rattling was all about, or they understood but were too absorbed in their own thoughts to care, or were moved to laughter and wanted to see more of the sideshow.

The boys immensely enjoyed Mr. Huncho's predicament but it was time to go before a cop came along. The miscreants broke up their group and moved away, leaving Mr. Huncho to the kindness of any passerby.

A few days after this incident, Dickron Stepanian had found another short–term job which helped him earn a few extra dollars to spend on groceries. He and Mariam, with their younger son in tow, purchased enough food to give them a holiday feeling. They left the grocery store and leisurely walked along the street. At first, they were unaware of the commotion behind them.

A bespectacled old–timer with a terrifying look was pushing pedestrians left and right to get ahead of them. He had recognized the boy holding his mother's hand. It was one of the gang members of the juvenile banditti trying to rob his candy store days before! Nothing would stop Mr. Huncho now.

Very rudely he pushed anyone ahead or to the side of him until he made a right of way for himself and closed the distance between himself and the couple with their boy. He roughly grabbed Dickron by the arm yanking him to the side. Alarmed by the assault, Dickron exclaimed, "Vot the hell you think you do?" as he pulled his arm free.

"Oh, you are Armenian?" asked Mr. Huncho.

"Yes, how did you know?"

"Your nose," said Mr. Huncho. "Please, I am not trying to be rude, but I must ask you. Are you this boy's father?"

"Yes, I am," Dickron answered, "but how do you know me?"

"Because I recognized your son," and Mr. Huncho got into a telling of the story of what had happened in his store. When he had finished and the boy had stopped trying to hide his face behind his mother's skirts, Dickron asked his son if what he had just heard was true. The boy hung his head and nodded yes.

By this time Mr. Huncho had talked most of his anger from

white hot to pale blue. "Oh, no," he said, in response to Dickron's question about possible damages, "it was a lot of trouble but no money involved. The next time you come by stop in and we will have some *soorj* [Armenian coffee]. I know you will do whatever needs doing to teach your boy what is right and wrong so he will know the difference."

"Thank you for your kind invitation," responded Dickron. "Yes. I will take care of this matter." Turning to his son he said, "Say you are sorry to this gentleman," and the boy apologized as he fought back the tears with bowed head. Dickron said to Mr. Huncho, "Thank you very much. I promise you a visit." They were not the best of friends yet, but friendship was on its way. When they said goodbye to each other and parted, Dickron told his son, "Here's a nickel. Buy some candy from Mr. Huncho and make sure you thank him for his kindness to you." Later that afternoon, father and son had a nice long talk about the whole incident.

In a few days, Harry's sweet tooth could no longer remain dormant. When it tingled enough he headed for the candy store with some trepidation, wondering how Mr. Huncho would receive him. When Mr. Huncho saw who it was he stood silently for a few moments, smiled, and said, "Vell, hello, young man, how are you, today," Harry knew everything was all right.

"I am very good, sir," Harry replied and Mr. Huncho smiled at the boy for finally addressing him with the title of respect that older men were entitled to. The smile on Mr. Huncho's face broadened. It was expected from children and Harry knew immediately that had he shown that courtesy the first time they'd met things might have been different.

"Vot vould you like, my boy," Mr. Huncho asked Harry, who seemed to lose his voice. When he finally found it and felt more secure he walked very slowly past the showcase and asked what he could have for four cents, which is all he had. Mr. Huncho saw the look on the boy's face and guessed the problem.

"Vie you not buy double ice cream cone?" he asked the boy.

"I don't have that much money," he answered.

"Never mind how much money. You vant ice cream, yes or no?" Mr. Huncho said with a big smile and handed Harry a chocolate–covered bar. Harry hesitated and Mr. Huncho said,

"That will be four cents," which Harry handed him with glee and said, "Wowie, thank you," again and again.

A month or two later, when the boy was in that neighborhood again, he went by the store and read a crude sign on the window which said, "Out of Business Sale." The boy felt as though someone had plunged a dagger in his heart like he had seen in the movies, only his pain felt a lot more real.

Harry's pain was forgotten as soon as his parents announced the family was going to the Pavlu picnic sponsored by the committee of those who had survived the massacres from that region. Harry and Garo were invited to go in such a way that they could not refuse. They were thrilled at the prospect of riding in one of the chartered buses that provided transportation to the event, held on a local farm.

When the Stepanians disembarked from their bus, the music and dancing had already started and the ladies were performing a sedate dance. They held hands in a large circle, took a sideways step to the right, crossed their feet to the right, then left, then a step back, then forward on the next step, then three rapid steps and so on. The applause was generous when the music and dance were completed.

Then two men stepped out, the music started again and the men began to move around each other in a slow, cautious circle, each man waving a cane overhead and holding a shoe over one hand as a shield. While slowly waving their canes at each other, they were both looking for the opening.

One of the men, with the speed of lightning over Mt. Ararat, swung at his opponent, who caught the blow on his shoe and tried to return it more effectively. The man who quit first lost the bout as soon as he hollered, "Enough." This was easy to do after several welts and bruises. All the men who had finished their fights joined in a dance. They held each other by the shoulders and formed a large circle, slowly dancing to the rhythm of tambourine and bagpipe. The exuberant audience kept time to the music with foot tapping and hand clapping.

Some of the patrons had brought their own lunches. Many of them purchased shish kebob sandwiches which was the real treat of the day. The rotisserie was about two feet wide, six feet long and held glowing charcoal in a trough about six inches deep. It took three men to do the barbecue of lamb.

Douglas Avenue

The meat was thoroughly trimmed of all fat, cut into one- or two-inch cubes, usually marinated the previous day.

Hollywood movies often showed skewers loaded with meat along with green peppers, eggplant, onions, and tomatoes in alternating fashion, all on the same skewers. It looked great in the movies but it wasn't practical in reality. At the picnic, vegetables of the same kind were placed on their own separate skewers since one kind of vegetable cooked more or less quickly than any other. Once roasted, the meat and vegetables were garnished with minced raw onions and parsley, and loaded inside pita pocket bread for eager customers. The aroma, wafting from the sizzling-hot roasted meat was so delicious it was "easy to eat one's fingers with it" as the vernacular had it.

The boys were ecstatic at the water pump. They took turns fighting for the pump handle and pumping with abandon until a pond was created into which some of them jumped to see who could make the biggest splash around their feet. They would worry later about what their mothers might say.

The adults continued their dancing, playing cards or backgammon, and chatting with neighbors whom they had not seen for a while until two or three speakers called for attention and said what had been said several times during picnics of the past few years. Then the dance music began all over again until soon it started getting dark and the time had arrived to go home.

It had been a typical Sunday of freedom from the worries and anxieties about the coming week, an opportunity to regain their strength to fight for life no matter what lay ahead. After all, these were the people who had survived the last attempt to wipe them off the earth's surface. The more their enemies or adversity threatened to wipe them out, the harder they lived to survive.

Years later, Adolf Hitler would ask, "Who today remembers the Armenians?" No other people of the twentieth century paid the same price and were more quickly forgotten than the "starving Armenians," as they were called. Yet, today the children and grandchildren of that earlier generation thrive and take with them into the future the wealth of their Armenian inheritance.

Chapter 18
The Skeletal Horse

Antro lived a few blocks away from the Stepanians. He was twenty years old, which helped the younger kids think he was an old man. At least he was old enough to drive an old paint–chipped Ford, which was on its last legs or wheels depending on how one viewed it. Antro spent much time constantly repairing one or another part of the jalopy.

On occasion he drove past the kids pitching horseshoes on the vacant lot across the street from the Whipple Street corner. He waved at them as they shouted greetings in his direction. He called them the Hoople Street Gang. The kids laughed because that's the way it was pronounced by the older generation of immigrants since they could not pronounce the "w" sound at the beginning of a word. It always came out sounding like the "v" sound. Hence, *wait* sounded like "vate," or "oo–ate." He had the kids mispronouncing it deliberately the same way when they shouted back, "Antro, vare you go?" and laughed.

One lovely day, Antro was driving by when he noticed Garo sighting in for his horseshoe pitch. He waved his hand, beckoning Garo to come over. Garo was proud to greet Antro, who said that he had some good news for Garo. He knew that Garo collected and mounted butterflies and dragonflies. He also knew of the good collection of seashells Garo owned.

"How would you like to have the skeleton of a horse?" Antro asked.

"A what of a what?" Garo asked in astonishment.

Antro laughed and repeated his question. Then he explained that he had seen a complete horse skeleton in the underbrush driving past it on a rain–soaked dirt trail outside of town, where he had spun his wheels out in the mud and almost failed to get his jalopy out on safer ground. It was a deal too good to be true, Garo thought. They agreed to meet on the morrow. Later that afternoon Garo went to the library and found a book on horses with pictures of complete skeletons with all parts nicely labeled. He drew two or three sketches of them before the library closed.

Early on the following morning they drove to the site. Garo agreed that the skeletal remains were in good condition only having turned light gray in color after who knew how many rains and snows had bleached them. They gathered the bones and made three trips to get them home and unloaded in the cellar with no one the wiser. Garo asked, "How much do I owe you? I'll pay you as soon as I can."

Antro replied, "You don't owe me nothin'. It's my gift to you. Okay?"

"Gee thanks!" Garo exclaimed.

It took Garo nearly four days after school to make preparations for putting things together. He collected odd lengths and diameters of iron pipe which had been lying around for ages, scrap lumber, several gallon bottles of bleach water, wire brushes, a hand drill with a variety of drill bits and odds and ends with which to start his undertaking.

On the fourth afternoon, Garo started a fire in the woodstove in the basement and proceeded to set some bones to boil for a while in a bleach bath, to sterilize and whiten them. In fifteen minutes or so, the heat and acrid fumes got to be too much as Garo salvaged the first batch from his mother's enameled turkey roaster and dumped more bones in the bath. By this time, he felt a strange burning sensation in his throat. He rushed to open the windows to let the fumes drift out, then dashed upstairs and out the door. Once outside, Garo sucked fresh air into his lungs and immediately felt better. Sometime later, he sneaked downstairs again and sniffed the air cautiously. This time, he felt his throat was a little less on fire.

He had processed a few more such bone batches when he heard his mother calling him. He shouted, "Yes, Momma, I'll be there in a minute," stretching that minute as long as he could.

"My son," Mariam shouted again in a louder voice, "what are you doing downstairs? What is that funny smell?"

"I'm repairing *Equus americani,*" he shouted back instantly, with the only response he could invent in a split second. It seemed to work, however, since there was a dumbfounded silence which seemed to last awhile.

Then Garo heard his mother, say, "I didn't understand you. What did you say you're doing?"

In the few moments of silence which followed, Garo quietly sneaked upstairs and slammed the outside door hard enough so that she might hear it. Meanwhile, his mother suddenly thought she smelled the green peppers burning, which were roasting and popping on the stove, and she rushed to rescue them.

Before noon Mariam had to leave for the neighbor's house. She had promised to teach her how to make stuffed and rolled cabbage leaves in Constantinople style. She would be gone for some three hours or more, she said, which was a mistake. Garo ran downstairs and started the fire again, chuckling at his good fortune when she left. Only this time he opened the window while he worked. He finished his task before his mother returned. This time the upstairs and downstairs were sufficiently aerated.

For the next several days Garo cut and bent the pipe lengths to size according to the diagrams he had drawn. On the fourth day, he cut and threaded the pipe ends with his father's threader and wrenched the pipes into their sockets. Two hours later he had wrenched the nipples into place with their corresponding sockets and then threaded the skull into place and halfway down he completed the attachment of the neck bones. He decided he had done enough to call it a day. Besides, he had noticed the anger in his mother's voice when she shouted she would not call again for him to come upstairs and there was no point in pushing his luck.

After dinner Harry walked with Garo who was headed toward Leonard's Pond with his butterfly net. He thought it best to stay away from the cellar for a day or two, frustrating though it might be. He was worried though that his mother was getting suspicious about the cellar and thought it best to steer her off the track.

It was Garo's mother who now got nervous. She was quite aware that something had been going on for a while downstairs but had carefully avoided opening the door to go down. It was no doubt poor judgment on her part because she knew it would take some doing. She steeled her nerve and opened the door and immediately noticed that the shade on the window downstairs must be drawn because it was dark enough to make her step down into the greater darkness with uncertainty.

The stairs were not only steep and dark but she had rarely used them before, but with the boys gone she would not have a better opportunity. She decided to risk it. She took two steps and entered the Stygian darkness. She waved her hand overhead hoping to feel the cord tied to the light bulb chain. She felt it at last and gave a gentle tug. For a brief moment the light blinded her and then she saw it—the dull gleam reflecting off the bleached skull was a ghastly sight to behold even for the briefest moment and so unexpected that she let out a terrified scream at the top of her lungs. She felt her legs grow weak and she grabbed the railing, which broke her fall. Her legs buckled as the world around her spun in a circle and she blacked out in a faint.

How long she lay with her body twisted in a heap she did not know but as her consciousness returned slowly she knew one of her legs could not bear the full weight of her body when she tried to push herself up to her feet. What was worse was her fear of the gruesome skull of the horse with its bare teeth grinning at her, or so it seemed to the dear lady. She managed to pull herself up by clinging to the railing, then slowly struggled up the stairs and limped to her bedroom. Mariam didn't know how long she lay in bed, gritting her teeth in distress. Her ankle was swollen, her knees bruised and her whole body ached. Mariam's ribs on her left side hurt so much whenever she shifted her position, that she suspected one or more of them might be cracked. Exhausted by pain, and her fearful experience, she finally fell asleep.

Sometime later, when she awakened, she saw her husband Dickron seated at the edge of the bed. He knew instantly that something was very wrong. He stroked her forehead and when her eyes began to flutter he gently asked, "My beloved, what has happened?" He leaned over and kissed her.

She smiled faintly and said, "I don't want you to get angry with Garo but I don't know how much of this I can take from the boys anymore."

"What did they do?" he asked.

"This time it was Garo," she said with tears filling her eyes. With her husband's encouragement, she started from the beginning. "Dearest man," she said, "I have never been so frightened. Those boys just won't stop and you must help me to have them understand. I just cannot put up with this much longer." She sobbed with pain as she kicked off her shoe and lifted her skirt to her knees.

Her husband winced when he saw the swollen bruises and discolored flesh. The full significance of what she had experienced hit home. He hugged her and said, "Don't worry. I will take care of this, I promise you."

"Don't forget you said you would not get angry with Garo."

"I won't forget," he said. "I gave you my word. Have I ever broken my word to you when I promised you anything?"

"No my man," she said, "truly you never have," as he leaned over, kissed her and straightened out her bed covers.

Dickron left the room and went to the cellar. When he saw the partially completed skeleton he admitted to himself that so far as it had gone it was a pretty good reconstruction of a horse. He also admitted that he could understand why his wife, raised in the city of her birth, would be petrified by what she had seen.

It was about time for dinner so he called the boys indoors and as they seated themselves at the table, they wondered aloud where their mother was. Their father said he would explain as soon as they had dinner, which consisted of bread and canned, store-bought red beans and that was all. Now the boys understood that something was seriously wrong with Momma and for the first time in their lives they felt a loneliness which they could not explain.

When they finished what passed for dinner, their father called them outside so that Momma would not be disturbed. It was then that he told them what had happened to Momma. "She made me promise not to punish you although we know how much you deserve it, but I promised her and must keep my word," he said.

"But I know nothing about what happened to Momma," said Garo.

"And neither do I," said Harry.

"It's not what either of you know or don't know," Poppa

interrupted. "It's what you did or didn't do," he added. "Had either of you told your mother that there was a pile of bare bones in the cellar she would have stayed away from there and her accident would never have happened."

"I am sorry, Poppa," Harry said. "It's my fault. I knew about the pile of bones because I had gone down cellar twice in Garo's absence but I said nothing because I knew he didn't want me to know or he would have told me otherwise, so I..."

"What did you just say ..." Garo exploded at the revelation. "You betrayed me!"

"That's enough! Both of you." Harry saw his mistake in saying too much.

"It's not what you said or didn't say. It's what you didn't do! Neither of you told your mother about that miserable pile of bones. Had you done so this terrible accident would not have occurred," Poppa reiterated. "All either of you were interested in was your miserable selfish motive and desire to do what you wanted and you see what that has done to your mother who, despite her pain and suffering, asked me not to punish you. She didn't think of herself first. She thought of you. Now, then. Garo, you tell me where you intend to display your museum piece."

There was no answer. Poppa broke the silence. "I'll tell where it'll go on display — at the city dump! I want both of you to help me tomorrow to load those bones so we can take them to the dump. Garo, I hate to say that and I know what it means to you but what your mother said has my approval. You cannot have it both ways so it's either Momma or the bones, and you know who I think comes first. I know you will agree when you think it over. Now go upstairs and apologize to her. This evening, I am going to Mr. Barsam's house to ask him what he will charge me for hauling us and those bones to the dump. I have nothing more to say."

Chapter 19
The First Round

Garo and Harry had gone to the scratch–house movie theater, enjoyed a Tom Mix feature and were walking home when it happened. About ten or twelve kids, some black and some white, had joined forces for a gang fight against the whole world, it seemed. They were looking for trouble.

The gang of boys, boisterous, threatening, and in a violent mood, suddenly appeared through the brush in front of Garo and Harry. Who knows why? It was just one of those days when anything that could have gone wrong did go wrong. The brothers instantly felt that something bad was about to happen. The gang formed a circle around the brothers and one of them stepped out in front, turned around and said to his followers "Hey, fellas, look at what we have here—a couple of these damned foreigners. Who told you that you could come here?" he snarled at the brothers.

"Nobody told us anything. We were just going home. That's all," Garo calmly responded.

"Oh, that was all, was it?" jeered the hulking boy who seemed to be the big boss. "Hey, guys," he shouted," this punk thinks he's a smart aleck. What shall we do with him?"

"Let me have him so I can teach him a lesson!" someone else shouted and soon everyone was shouting that he wanted to get into the act.

The apparent leader of the show was waving his hands for quiet so he could be heard. Garo realized that as Harry's older brother, it was his responsibility to protect him and he had to think and act quickly. There was no way he and Harry could avoid a fight so he had to come up with a spur–of–the–moment strategy to ensure their survival by increasing the odds in their favor. He had to steer the whole thing to his advantage. He exerted enough pressure on the "boss man" in order to gain enough attention to take the lead. He stole the act from the lead man by shouting, "I'll fight in my kid brother's place!" Immediately the controversy subsided. The gang waited for direction from the boss man and Garo knew to whom, in the meantime, he could interject what was on his mind.

"Look," he said to the boss man, "you look like a sport. I can't believe that you expect me, or my kid brother, to fight your whole gang. How about your letting me pick out an opponent of my choice and let us slug it out. Let the best man win. Okay?" There may have been some fear in his voice but there was no bluff.

Garo had recognized one of the group in front of him. He was the grandson of one of the old–timers from Italy whose family lived on Federal Hill, better known as Little Italy. Garo took charge. He felt some fear of the gang, no doubt about it, but he forced himself to carry out the plan which had entered his mind when the whole confrontation had begun.

Garo had chosen his target carefully. The Italian kid was the tallest—and biggest–looking guy in the bunch and he looked like a giant compared to all the other kids. On two or three occasions Garo had seen him walking in North Providence and there was no problem in ever recognizing him again. It was in the way he walked. When he took a step forward it seemed as though he quickly raised himself to his toes. This made him look as though he had stepped on some live coals and he couldn't get his feet off the fire soon enough. It made him look like a Felix the Cat cartoon where his rear end was too slow catching up to his front end.

For all his formidable size, Garo's chosen opponent was clumsy and Garo guessed that his own quick reflexes would give him the advantage in a fight. So Garo pointed toward the boy, exclaiming, "I choose to fight this guy," and pointed to Rocco.

"Okay," agreed the boss and the other gang members shouted their approval and began shoving Rocco toward the front of the group. Knowing that they wouldn't have to fight today, Rocco's fellow gang members were suddenly full of bravado, yelling words of encouragement and advice at him.

"Knock him out," screamed one. "He's nothing but a pansy!"

In unison now, the boys clamored, "Yeah, Rocco, kill the bastard!"

The First Round

Garo and Rocco suddenly found themselves in a small clearing surrounded by all the other boys. Rocco made the first move, delivering a glancing blow to Garo's jaw and the onlookers erupted with cacophonous joy.

Garo skipped a step or two, feinted, ducked low to let another punch cut the air in two over his head and swiveled around before he threw a counterpunch at Rocco's jaw. It was a solid, bone–crunching smash which rocked Rocco backward and before he could regain his balance, Garo landed two more rapid jaw crunchers before he danced backward with agility. Another couple of feints and Garo closed in again with another couple of lightning–quick jabs and Rocco, peering through glazed eyes, staggered backward, with one hand behind him as though feeling for something to lean against. "Look," urged Garo, "you're nearly finished now. Do you want to quit?"

"No!" drawled Rocco and stepped forward, throwing another wild punch which connected with wide–open emptiness.

"Please quit," Garo pleaded. "I don't want to hurt you any more," and spread both arms as Rocco swayed into them. Only then did Garo realize that the dampness he felt was a trickle of blood running down Rocco's nose.

"Hey, you sucker," Garo shouted to the boss man, "come and get your boy!" as he lowered Rocco to the ground. "He's twice the man you'll ever be," he shouted loudly enough for the gang to hear. It worked, because the gang started edging away, as he'd hoped they would.

As Rocco managed to stagger to his feet, Garo saw a smile of sheer gratitude crossing his bloody face. Garo leaned toward Rocco and whispered, "You've got more guts than that whole bunch of cowards, and I respect you for that." Garo thought he saw Rocco's face light up just before he passed out and slumped to the ground again.

The wild man who only moments before had been boldly hurling taunts and obscenities in Garo's direction, was now making a move to sneak away when he heard Harry speaking to him directly. "I should have told you," Harry said, "that my brother knows boxing. If you'd like to try him out, that is if you're not too scared, then stand your ground and don't run away like a rabbit." The boss man blanched and redoubled his efforts to make his escape.

Chapter 20
Tony's Spaghetti Parlor

Saturday afternoons would find two or three of the boys discussing which Western cowboy heroes to see at the movies. As the group grew larger, so did the discussions. There was a treasure trove of some of the greatest stars for the juvenile crowd. Tom Mix, Buck Jones, Ken Maynard, Bob Steele, Hoot Gibson, Johnny Mack Brown, Jack Hoxie, Tom Tyler, George O'Brien, Yakima Canutt, and Tim McCoy were among the most popular. The kids, sooner or later, got into serious arguments about who the best cowboys were. It was no surprise that their choices bore a resemblance to the way they thought they resembled the actor. A word or scowl or grin was enough to get a label pinned on the kid.

Hampo (Hairabedian) became Tim McCoy for his blue eyes; Kelly (Kaloustian) became Bob Steele for his slim, toothy smile; Chocko (Chokoian) was Hoot Gibson for the way he nodded his head before speaking; Garo Stepanian for his broad, silent smile became Ken Maynard; Harry Stepanian was George O'Brien because he was husky, tough, fiery and so on. It was not a problem when the boys got tired of the names. When private detectives, buccaneers, gangsters, U.S. marshals and other roles became popular, the kids just changed their identities from previous roles and started all over again.

Usually, the kids went over to the "scratch house" or the movies at the second–run theatres on Saturdays which showed two Westerns plus serials plus selected shorts. All this for ten cents for a seat upstairs on benches that had four advantages: first, it was cheaper at ten cents for admission; second, some ushers would look the other way when the kids smuggled in their bag lunches prepared by their mothers in advance and this allowed the kids to watch the feature picture twice and eat heartily at the same time; third, the benches nearest the second floor railings made it easier to aim popcorn down on the patrons below; fourth, the culprits had sufficient time to pass their bags to their buddies in back of them, who would quickly hide the popcorn in the semidarkness before the ushers dashed upstairs to find the culprits who were pretending well–mannered innocence with their popcorn. Then, the kids who had bought a bag or two of jelly beans passed them around to their ogling chums.

Double–feature movies were coming into vogue and the first movie shown,usually a romance, was always considered a flop by the kids. They sat through the movie, talking, laughing and jeering until the Westerns came on with the stage coaches, blazing six–shooters and trick horses. (One of them always untied the knots with which the good guy had been tied up by the bad guys.) The fist fights were always won by the good guys who fought clean, teaching the kids a sense of fairness. There was always the fist fight where the bad guy was punched so hard against the china hutch that it was knocked over, with the dishes always crashing to the floor. Once, the good guy saw a moving reflection on the back of the whiskey bottle of the villain coming at him from behind. Without turning around, the hero drew his six–shooter, and firing backward over his shoulder, shot the villain dead. He holstered his gun in a wink and picked up his guitar, twanging it without missing a note. Now that was some shooting and the kids broke out first with laughter and then applause. The good guys drew guns quicker and their aim was phenomenal. They leaped down from the rooftop and landed on the horse without fracturing the back of the beast.

The heroes always knew the bad guy was after the old widow's oil and she didn't know it was right under the house. Also, the lovely young lady's cattle had been rustled to the other side of the canyon and she didn't know that either. But the good guys always found out, shot the guilty parties and made restitution, because honesty was the best policy. The heros never mistreated women and lovely lassies. They never let their hands wander to the wrong places. The kids always knew the bad guy was the one with the black, narrow mustache; there was no vulgarity from anyone including the dance hall floozies, and the good guys always stood up and said, "Pardon me, ma'am," for not having stood up with courtesy soon enough.

On the silver screen, when the bad guy was just about ready to shoot, one of the kids always beat him to the shot by shooting a cap pistol in the theatre, at which moment the boys cheered and the ushers looked vainly for the miscreant. At the very end of the movie, the good cowboy gave the beautiful young lady a chaste kiss, at which Garo led the boys to boo their feigned disgust so that none would think they were sissies.

The kids didn't go to the first–run movies simply because their parents couldn't afford it. However, on occasion, Harry and Chocko successfully sneaked into the high–class theatres. When they returned home they told tales to the gang that were hard to believe and it had little to do with the movie, but with the theatre itself. They described the glittering chandeliers, rich lodges, velvet curtains, luxurious carpeting, marbled foyers, ormolu fittings, ornately carved woodwork, and a look of overwhelming splendor. Right then and there is when some of the kids suddenly learned what their poverty was really like and vowed to escape it when they grew up, and some of them did in a big way when the time arrived. They received the inspirations first seen in theatres like Fay's, Lowe's State, Majestic, Albee, Strand, and others.

Several of the kids worked hard to scrape up the twenty-five cents admission fee to see all this in the first–class theaters. They had to be more careful about sneaking in with the bag lunches but the coast was clear during intermission time. That's when the lights came on and people got up to walk to the lobby and the concession stands to buy popcorn, soda, and candy. The patrons were so busy walking around, or into, each other they did not notice what the kids were doing.

The first–run theatres showed only one feature picture but these were the movie palaces showing off incredibly fantastic and beautiful interiors with vaudeville intermissions, slapstick comedians, stage stunts, and dances. It was also time for the huge electric organ to rise mysteriously through the stage floor at Fay's and someone dressed in a tuxedo was always seated at the organ. He would play the popular songs of the day while the patrons watched the projected moving ball on the screen bouncing up and down in rhythm with the music to tell the audience which words it should be singing at any one moment. That's when the kids slowly unwrapped their lunches and wolfed them down before being seen. The audience was too hypnotized, swaying in rhythm with music and song and bobbing heads, to watch the kids' antics or to notice the ushers' absence. The latter had sneaked away to the men's room for a smoke.

In 1931, the movie *Frankenstein* was a stunning success setting the stage for the horror films of the times and the good ones were works of art. To see Karloff do his thing was worth the extra cost, if the kids had to pay for it, because they would enjoy being scared out of their wits. Karloff was worth the wait.

For days afterward, the kids would drag their feet, walking as if they were heavily weighted down so as to get the same effect Karloff had achieved. They didn't know that he really wore a seven–pound shoe on each foot in the filming of the movie. They got a pretty decent result, however, when they twisted their mouths in such a way as to produce the awful, "Arrr, urrgh," the monster gargled as he ripped the air with his gnarled, menacing hands.

After the movie, the gang walked out across the street to Tony's Spaghetti Parlor for meatball sandwiches, which were huge and smothered in tomato sauce with garlic. Not every kid had the dime for it but another who did would share with him. One time, to their surprise, the lunch counter was closed and there was a notice fastened to the plate glass window. It was in technical language but it boiled down to saying the place was closed by the order of the Board of Health. What had happened? The newspaper reported it in a few days. The tank–bellied restaurateur who always smiled and greeted the kids had been arrested for mixing canned dog food with the meatballs. The newspaper accounts said he had paid only two cents a can for the meat. His statement to the press was that the ground meatball mix was healthy food high in protein and he had not heard any complaints so far. Confused by all they'd heard, the kids were certain of one fact: for a dime, his jumbo–size sandwich could be equaled by no one else's in town.

The kids were genuinely sorry. They had eaten many of

those delicious sandwiches for at least a couple of years and no one had suffered any ill effects. To be sure, there had been some complaints by two boys who always complained about everything. Neither had seen a doctor, so where was the proof? There may have been a case or two of distemper but no one from the gang, at least, came forth to admit it after rumors spread on Douglas Avenue that any stool pigeon who had squawked to the press and spilled the beans would pay for it with black eyes. Nobody else made such delicious meatballs and Tony was too nice a guy, who would never do anything like what he was accused of doing.

The boys knew that something important was missing from their lives. It was Tony with his rotundity, mellow voice, and memories of the silver screen the boys missed. He had become a symbol of carefree boyhood, which was quickly coming to an end during those troubled times. The boys could not forget him easily. Years later, when the boys ran into each other as grown men, they often reminisced and laughed about how delicious Tony's notorious meatball sandwiches had tasted. Nobody knew what happened to him.

Chapter 21
The Nickel Shoe Shine

Garo noticed a change on Douglas Avenue. Three or four of the usual gang had gathered there and to his surprise, Garo noticed that they were kneeling in front of homemade shoe-shine boxes. Each boy would dab shoe polish on a customer's shoes, and brush them to a good shine, then snapping a polishing cloth with a professional flourish, produce a finishing polish before calling for the next patron. There were two or three others waiting their turns. Garo stopped long enough to say hello to Mickey, one of the best baseball players in the gang, to find out what was going on. It was a pleasant surprise to see him and the others at work and making money at it.

Garo learned that a small group of them went there on Saturday mornings and set up shop in front of a vacant store. The boys were open for business from about nine in the morning until about noon. Garo was surprised he had not known about the enterprise. "How long has this been going on?" he asked Mickey.

"Oh, since last summer," Mickey answered and asked his customer for the other foot and said to Garo, "If you want to join us why don't you show up next Saturday?"

Before Garo could answer, Mickey's customer asked with irritation, "Are you two gonna gab all day or will you finish doing my shoes?"

"Yes, sir. I'm sorry. Right away," Mickey answered and to Garo he added, "I'll see you later."

Garo went on the search for material, found some wooden box ends and went to work the following day. It didn't take long to put his shine box together and he was especially glad for the way in which the footrest turned out. Then he selected some of his father's tins of shoe paste and had to buy only a few additional tools of the trade. The rest he begged from his mother. Then he busied himself with chores around the yard and waited with impatience for Saturday morning. He adjusted his shoulder straps on the shoe-shine box, headed down Douglas Avenue toward the drugstore, and hummed a jolly tune to himself.

Garo heard some grumbling among the shoe shiners since business was slower than usual. In fact, two of the boys were playing cards while the other three, not including Garo, were trying to keep a conversation from dying into silence. Before long, the boys began to disperse and the shoe-shine crew disappeared—all but Garo. Soon enough he had a feeling of despondency. Any joyous thoughts he'd had only a few moments before disappeared. The pedestrians also disappeared and the avenue seemed devoid of all life. He slumped against the lamppost and lost himself in troubled thoughts. The passage of time seemed endless and empty.

What finally pushed him into full awareness was the screeching of metal as a flashy convertible, with top down, came to a sudden stop. Including the driver, there were seven youths and all of them were nattily dressed, each wearing a silk necktie and custom-tailored suit. Garo guessed they were in their twenties and probably from the east side of town where all the money had always been.

The young man who reached Garo first asked if he was open for business and Garo jumped up with a "Yes, sir" and placed a cushion on the step for a seat. He couldn't believe his good luck. The young customer was a token for what followed. As Garo put the finishing touches on the Cordovan shoe leather, a couple of the customer's chums gathered around to watch.

"What do I owe you, kid," the customer asked, critically admiring the shine and admitting to himself that it was a very good one, indeed.

"How about a dime?" Garo asked. "I gave you a real good shine didn't I?"

"A dime?" the customer asked and Garo's heart sank. He thought his audacity in asking for twice as much as the going rate was a great blunder despite the truth that he really had put in a lot more effort and time than usual.

"A dime?" asked the man, again. "You'll never get rich working that hard for so little. Here, take this. You really earned it, so why are you selling yourself so short?" he asked and flipped a quarter into Garo's outstretched hand. Garo stood almost paralyzed when he saw how much money he was given and the gentleman said, "Keep the change."

One of the gentleman's pals sauntered over and asked his buddy what was taking so long and holding things up. "I just asked the kid to take his time and give me a good shine. Isn't it a beauty?" he asked, lifting and wiggling his foot.

"Yeah," the new arrival replied "but the guys are waiting."

"I'll go tell them to wait some more since you're here. Why don't you guys get a shine and don't be afraid to spend a little money." He winked at his chums and waved them forward as he walked toward the parked automobile. He told them that their buddy was coming as soon as he got his shine. "Shall I tell the shoe-shine boy that you guys will show up next?"

"Well, why not," one of them said. "We'll all get a shine so nobody will think that the rest of us are cheapskates. By the way, what is he charging?"

"What does it matter," one of them piped up. "Your old man has enough money to pay for the whole city block," and they all pitched in with loud guffaws and agreement.

When the fellows left the auto and walked over to Garo's shoe–shine stop it occurred to him that he'd better put some moxie in it, which was the latest "in" phrase of the vernacular for a popular soft drink. One of the customers asked again what it cost and Garo said the last man had given him twenty–five cents and when the man who asked was told that, he let out a soft whistle of procrastination. "But you can give me whatever you want," Garo said. It was a master stroke of financial wizardry although Garo had not intended it that way.

One of the young men said to the last speaker, "Jimmie, don't be a freeloader and give the kid what he was last paid. After all, you asked for it and he set the standard."

"Yeah, yeah!" someone else shouted and soon enough they upped the ante when two of the boys pitched in fifty cents, each. They wanted fame and glory and were glad to pay for it. Jimmie was one of the two spendthrifts and had the satisfaction of wiping out the competition according to his way of thinking. Unwittingly, Garo had established whatever the market would bear in the true spirit of capitalism because no one wanted to be a cheapskate.

When the young men finally got seated in the car, they were all looking at each other's footwear to see who had the brightest shine although no one wanted to start a fight over it. Garo sat down for a few minutes when he was satisfied he had counted his total earnings correctly at two dollars and twenty–five cents. He had never earned so much money anytime and he was thrilled. He finally walked his weary way home knowing he would have to build some kind of comfortable folding chair for his customers.

But when he entered his house all fatigue seemed to disappear. When Mariam, who had no inkling where her son had been for nearly four hours, asked him for an explanation, he grinned broadly and asked if he could talk in the presence of his father. His mother knew something unusual must have happened. First, she told her son to wash his face and hands clean of dirty smudges, which she couldn't identify. Then she called her husband to come indoors. "Man, please come in from the garden. Your son and I need to talk to you."

When he had dusted himself off and entered the kitchen, Dickron asked, "What is the matter?"

"Well, son, here is your father. Will you talk, now?" Mariam asked.

Garo said, still grinning, "Oh, well, it's not so important, I guess," as he reached into his pocket, pulled out a fistful of change and casually dumped it on the table.

"Good heavens!" Mariam gasped over the jingling of the silver coins.

Dickron narrowed his eyelids and in a clipped voice asked, "All right, son, what is the meaning of all this, eh?"

"Nothing much, Poppa," Garo said, enjoying the role with which he was teasing his parents. "Some of my buddies had invited me to go to their stomping grounds where they shine shoes so I went, too. There was little business today. All the guys quit early except me. I got lucky when a car full of rich-looking guys pulled their car over and they paid me more than I asked for. Now I must ask you for a kindness. I want you, Poppa, to have this for you

The Nickel Shoe Shine

and Momma." With pride, Garo pushed the coins across the table to his father.

"Wait a minute," Dickron said. "What are you doing?"

"I am asking you to take this gift from me to you and Momma for all the things you have both done for me," Garo explained.

There was a moment of silence and his father said, "Excuse me," coughed, and covering his mouth with his hankie, he hurried to the bathroom, coughing all the while.

"What's the matter with Poppa?" Harry asked.

"I think he's getting a bad cold," Mariam said. "I'd better check on him."

She got up, went over and knocked on the door, and entered, quickly shutting it behind her. Her husband's eyes were wet with tears as she put her arms around his shoulder and whispered, "Dearest man, don't cry, please don't cry." She gently wiped the tears from his eyes and said, "We'll wait for you. It is not a shame for you to accept the money your son gives to you as a sign of his love for you."

"What's the matter with Poppa?" both boys asked simultaneously when their mother reappeared.

"I think he's developing a bad cold," Mariam suggested and Harry said, "I bet..." and Garo kicked his brother in the shin and brought on the silence for which Dickron was grateful as he returned. The boys had never seen their father cry out of shame or gratitude and they did not see him cry now. Quickly, Mariam introduced a new topic of conversation just long enough for Dickron to regain his composure.

"May I bring you a cup of mint tea?" his wife asked him.

"Yes, please," he replied, and looking at Garo, "Thank you, my son, for your gift."

"Son," Mariam said, "we are going to visit the Kevorkians and want you and your brother to go with us."

"Aw, gee, Momma," Harry said, "we have a ball game with the Fillmore gang and the boys really are expecting me. Can't I go?" he pleaded.

Mariam looked at her husband and said, "It's all right by me if your father agrees," and he discreetly nodded, giving her the support she wanted.

Harry jumped to his feet saying, "Thank you, Poppa, thank you, Momma," and grabbed his glove and charged outside.

127

"Well," Dickron asked his wife, "what do you want us to do?"

"We promised the Kevorkians we would visit them unless you've changed your mind," she said.

From the way she said it, he knew she really wanted to go. "Now, it's up to you," he said to Garo.

Garo sat silently for a minute, then replied, "Poppa, I'd really rather go to the Saturday matinee."

"Don't hesitate," his father said. "Is this enough?" he asked, pushing back two quarters.

"That's more than enough," Garo answered. "I want you and Momma to spend the rest on yourselves. I love you both."

"We love you, too," his parents responded.

Garo went into his bedroom and changed into his best clothes, then said "Goodbye," and left.

"What a beautiful boy he is," Mariam observed. "These are his first real earnings and see how gladly he has given them to us."

"Yes, I know," Dickron agreed. "Too bad we're committed to house visiting. I'll go, but tomorrow I look forward to honoring our son's request by taking you out for the evening—just the two of us."

Suddenly noting the far away look in his wife's eyes, Dickron asked, "What are you thinking about?"

"Doesn't it seem like yesterday that we met for the first time? That day on Ellis Island, I desperately searched for you among those who had arrived to greet their loved ones. I thought you'd never come for me. I waited for what seemed like an eternity, your photo gripped for dear life in my hand!"

"Yes, I was a little late that day," admitted Dickron.

"I hope you've never regretted marrying your picture postcard bride?" Mariam teased.

"Never! I remember when you first hinted in a letter that you wished you could come to America. I saw my opportunity, wrote and offered you fare for the voyage and my hand in marriage!"

"Could you imagine on our wedding day that we would be so blessed? We have two fine sons and a beautiful baby daughter. This is truly a land of milk and honey. Thank God, our children have a promising future," Mariam proclaimed with certainty and heartfelt gratitude.

www.ingramcontent.com/pod-product-compliance
Lightning Source LLC
Chambersburg PA
CBHW060838050426
42453CB00008B/737